FUNCHAL
Adegas de São Francisco
Casa Museu Frederico de Freitas
Convento de Santa Clara
Fortaleza de São Tiago
IBTAM
Madeira Story Centre
Mercado dos Lavradores
Museu de Arte Sacra
Museu A Cidade do Açúcar
Museu Henrique e Francisco Franco
Museu Municipal
Museu Photographia Vicentes
Quinta das Cruzes
Sé
Zona Velha

Faial

Porto da Cruz

101

Ponta de São Lourenço

Caniçal

EASTERN

Machico

Camacha

Santa Cruz

s do
ro

101

Garajau

TWINPACK
Madeira

MARC DI DUCA

AA Publishing
If you have any comments or suggestions for this guide you can contact the editor at
travelguides@TheAA.com

How to Use This Book

This guide is divided into four sections
• Essential Madeira: An introduction to the island and tips on making the most of your stay.
• Madeira by Area: We've broken the island into five areas, and recommended the best sights, shops, activities, restaurants, entertainment and nightlife venues in each one. Suggested walks and drives help you to explore.
• Where to Stay: The best hotels, whether you're looking for luxury, budget or something in between.
• Need to Know: The info you need to make your trip run smoothly, including getting about by public transport, weather tips, emergency phone numbers and useful websites.

Navigation In the Madeira by Area chapter, we've given each area its own colour, which is also used on the locator maps throughout the book and the map on the inside front cover.

Maps The fold-out map accompanying this book is a comprehensive map of Madeira. The grid on this fold-out map is the same as the grid on the locator maps within the book. The grid references to these maps are shown with capital letters (A1); those to the town plan are shown with lower-case letters (a1).

Contents

Introducing Madeira

The tip of an extinct volcano protruding from the Atlantic's sapphire surge, Madeira is a lush paradise of quaint fishing villages, whitewashed churches, jagged peaks and deep valleys, a dramatic backdrop for a relaxed but invigorating stay.

Some 900km (560 miles) from mainland Portugal and over 600km (370 miles) from the Moroccan coast, Madeira resembles neither. Towns and villages cling to coastal ledges while the volcano that gave birth to the island rises sheer from the ocean floor, culminating in cloud-ripping peaks over 1,800m (5,900ft) above sea level.

Once prosperous from the proceeds of sugar shipped to northern Europe, Madeira is now the recipient of a precious commodity sent in the other direction—plane-loads of holiday-makers. Tourism is a huge revenue generator for the island, creating jobs in hospitality and services as well as keeping many traditional handicrafts and cottage industries alive. Thousands of visitors, mainly from Britain, Germany and Scandinavia, jet in annually to escape the nippy northern winter or to hike the *levadas*, Madeira's unique system of aqueducts. Many retirees call the island home, in particular expats from Britain, with which Madeira has historical, cultural and trade links.

Although the island has imported sand, and has a few scraps of natural grey sand of its own, Madeira is not a beach destination. Its sister island of Porto Santo has a long stretch of golden strand, but otherwise pickings are meagre. Madeira is more about getting up into the mountains, hiking the *levadas*, motoring through the clouds to the top of peaks and taking buses up almost vertical roads to jaw-dropping vistas. It's about traditional handicrafts without the hard sell, gardens overflowing with subtropical vegetation, brightly painted fishing boats hauled up onto basalt shores, and terraces of vines and bananas sweetening under an Atlantic sun. And, when you've seen all this, you'll still make it back to Funchal for dinner.

Facts + Figures

- Madeira welcomes over a million visitors a year, including 180,000 from the UK.
- The Laurisilva (laurel) Forest has been a UNESCO World Heritage Site since 1999. Covering some 16 per cent of Madeira, it is the world's largest surviving laurel forest.

HAIL RONALDO

Arguably, Madeira's most famous son is the footballer Cristiano Ronaldo dos Santos Aveiro, Real Madrid *galáctico* and former Manchester United winger. Born in Funchal in 1985, Ronaldo began his career with the local team Nacional. His parents named him after Ronald Reagan.

THE ATLANTIS MYTH

Some writers have touted the theory that the Madeiran archipelago is the remnants of Atlantis, a legendary civilization said to have conquered Western Europe before sinking beneath the waves in a single day. No evidence has been found on the ocean floor to prove that a great empire ever existed above the surface, though it is an intriguing theory. It should also be said that many other locations in the Atlantic and Mediterranean also stake claims to the Atlantis legend.

FELLOW ISLANDS

Other islands in the Madeiran archipelago are Porto Santo, the only other inhabited island, 40km (25 miles) to the northeast, the Desertas, 26km (16 miles) offshore and dominating the view from Funchal, and the Selvagens, 300km (180 miles) to the south. Distant relatives include the Azores, 900km (560 miles) northwest, the Canary Islands, 450km (280 miles) south, and the Cape Verde Islands, a distant 1,800km (1,120 miles) south.

A Short Stay in Madeira

DAY 1: FUNCHAL

Morning Begin with a breakfast of traditional pastries and coffee at **Penha D'Aguia** (▷ 47) or **Grand Café Golden Gate** (▷ 46) to set you up for the morning's exploration. Your second stop should be the **Sé** (▷ 32), Madeira's cathedral with its Manueline decoration and impressively carved cedar ceiling inlaid with ivory. From there, head uphill to the **Convento de Santa Clara** (▷ 33) and pay your respects to Zarco, the Portuguese navigator who reputedly discovered Madeira. Nearby is the don't-miss **Quinta das Cruzes** (▷ 30), an old mansion-turned-museum packed with interesting island memorabilia and set in peaceful grounds with splashing fountains and mature trees.

Lunch Head down to **Armazém do Sal** (▷ 45), an atmospheric spot just off the seafront and ideal for a light seafood lunch or a more substantial Madeiran-Argentine fusion feast.

Afternoon Stroll around the **Museu de Arte Sacra** (▷ 28) before ambling along the seafront to the **Madeira Story Centre** (▷ 34) for a potted history of the island. You are now in the **Zona Velha** (▷ 36), Funchal's enchanting old quarter. Take atmospheric Rua de Santa Maria to the Largo do Corpo Santo, which has some of the island's oldest churches. The ochre hulk of the **São Tiago Fortress** (▷ 36) will stop you in your tracks before long; return along the seafront.

Dinner The Zona Velha is the place to head in the evening for food and local colour. **O Tapassol** (▷ 48) is especially memorable, not just for the superb Madeiran dishes but also for its understated decor.

Evening Book a table at **Arsenios** (▷ 45) where the Portuguese wines are accompanied by live *fado* music.

DAY 2: AROUND FUNCHAL

Morning Launch your day by gliding above Eastern Funchal in the cable car to **Monte** (▷ 58). Safely delivered more than 500m (1,640ft) above sea level, clamber up the steps of the historical church of **Nossa Senhora do Monte** (▷ 58), where you'll find the tomb of Charles I of Austria, who died in exile in Monte. Afterwards, enjoy a circuit of the lush **Monte Palace Gardens** (▷ 58), before hopping aboard a traditional wicker toboggan (▷ 59) for the slither down to Livramento. Bus it from here into central Funchal.

Lunch Squeeze into a seat at **Gavião Novo** (▷ 46), a tightly packed restaurant in the Zona Velha, for locally sourced lamb and fish.

Afternoon Climb aboard one of the regular buses from Funchal station to the atmospheric fishing village of **Câmara de Lobos** (▷ 53), famously captured on canvas by Winston Churchill. Join the local fishermen for a shot of *poncha* before hiking up to the top of **Cabo Girão** (▷ 52). Soak up the stupendous views then grab a coffee in the snack bar near the cliff edge. Taxis at Cabo Girão will whisk you onwards to **Ribeira Brava** (▷ 84) where an insight into traditional life and culture in the **Ethnographical Museum** and a look around the baroque **Church of St. Benedict** can be followed by a swim in the sea.

Dinner Pick one of the restaurants along Ribeira Brava's palm-lined promenade and enjoy some alfresco dining to the sound of waves crashing on the beach.

Evening A short bus or taxi hop along the motorway will take you back to Funchal, where you can end the day relaxing over drinks in one of the many local bars.

Top 25

TOP 25

▶ ▶ ▶

Adegas de São Francisco ▷ 26 Sample Madeiran wine and learn about its production in the island's oldest wine lodge.

Teleféricos ▷ 61 Float high above the roofs of old Funchal in Madeira's ultra-modern cable car.

Sé ▷ 32 Take a pew in Madeira's cathedral, a fine piece of Manueline architecture.

Santana ▷ 72 Peek into the unique A-frame houses on the main square and in the Madeira Theme Park on the outskirts of town.

Ribeiro Frio ▷ 70 For cool mountain air and fresh trout, head for this pretty village, the start of several *levada* walks.

Ribeira Brava ▷ 84 Stroll along the palm-fringed promenade of this seaside town, a short hop off the Funchal motorway.

Quinta das Cruzes ▷ 30 Glimpse how the island's upper classes once lived in this fine old *quinta*.

Porto Moniz ▷ 83 Dip your feet in natural sea pools, the main attraction at this northwest outpost.

Boca da Encumeada ▷ 66 This mountain pass has views of both the north and south coasts.

Cabo Girão ▷ 52 Enjoy panoramic views from some of the highest sea cliffs in the world.

Porto Moniz

Reserva Natural Integral

WESTERN 79-92

Boca da Encumeada

Parque Natural da Madeira

Calheta

Curral das Freiras

Ribeira Brava

Cabo Girão

Câmara de Lobos

Pico Ruivo ▷ 69 Climb to the top of Madeira's highest peak for stunning, cloud-wreathed panoramas.

Pico do Arieiro ▷ 68 Make an ascent of Madeira's third highest mountain—by car.

These pages are a quick guide to the Top 25, which are described in more detail later. Here they are listed alphabetically, and the tinted background shows which area they are in.

CENTRAL 63–78
Santana

1861 Pico Ruivo
Reserva Natural Integral
Ribeiro Frio
1805 Pico do Arieiro

EASTERN 93–106
Caniçal
Machico

SOUTHERN 49–62
Museu de Arte Sacra
Quinta das Cruzes
Monte
Teleféricos
Jardim Botânico
Camacha
Jardins do Palheiro
Mercado dos Lavradores

Casa Museu Frederico de Freitas
Sé
Adegas de São Francisco

FUNCHAL 20–48

◀ ◀ ◀

9

Out and About

The most popular activity on Madeira is hiking the *levadas* and mountain trails of the rugged interior. Every year thousands of people pull on boots and take up sticks to hike the paths running alongside the irrigation channels that crisscross the island. Once the only way to get around the island, the *levadas* offer a quintessentially Madeiran experience. Hikers are literally following in the footsteps of generations of hardy islanders.

What's a *Levada*?

A *levada* is a channel that funnels water from the wet interior of Madeira to its drier coasts. Preventing the 2m (79in) of rain that falls on the mountains annually from simply running off into the sea, the network of *levadas* provides a controllable water supply to small holdings, fish farms and even hydroelectric power plants. The first *levadas* were constructed by early settlers, and the last ones in the 1960s. Now there are around 2,000km (1,240 miles) of these concrete-lined aqueducts on the island. They are fundamental to Madeira's economy, not only to its agriculture but also to tourism; every year visitors from all over the world come to Madeira specifically to walk this unique piece of infrastructure.

Where to Start

Most *levada* walks head up into the mountains or down to the coast, but a few go cross-country, keeping at a high elevation all the way. The

Madeira's rugged coast and interior are famously green thanks to the network of levadas

---

THE *LAVADEIRO*

While tramping alongside the *levadas*, you may bump into a *levadeiro*, whose job is to repair and unblock the *levadas* when they become clogged with leaves and other debris and to open and close sluices, making sure the water is evenly distributed among those who need it. Many walkers envy the *levadeiro's* job, patrolling areas of natural beauty, but it's a very responsible role—a blunder by the *lavadeiro* can ruin crops and livelihoods.

vast majority are linear rather than circular, so it's usually best to use public transport rather than a rental car to reach the start of a walk and also to get back to your base at the end. Many trailheads are served by bus, and a taxi from Funchal to any point on the island doesn't cost a fortune.

Pick your Route

There are literally hundreds of *levada* walks and many different route combinations, so buying a specialist guide such as John and Pat Underwood's *Madeira Car Tours and Walks* is well worth doing if you want detailed guidance. Popular non-*levada* walks on the island include the hike down from Eira do Serrado to Curral das Freiras (▷ 55), the peak-to-peak walk from Pico do Arieiro to Pico Ruivo (▷ 68) and the epic slog from Pico Ruivo to Boca da Encumeada (▷ 69).

Don't Look Down

You'll certainly need a head for heights if you want to hike the *levadas*. Unprotected drops, sometimes plunging hundreds of metres to the valley floor, can unnerve even experienced walkers. Be sure to check the weather forecast before you set out and tell staff at your hotel where you are going and when you expect to return. Don't underestimate the temperature difference between the south coast and the interior, nor the risk of exposure should you be caught at high altitudes in bad weather without proper clothing (▷ below).

Elevated but flat, the levadas offer good walking and fabulous views over the lush landscape

---

GEARING UP

Experienced hikers will know exactly what to take on a foray into the wilds of Madeira. But if you've never donned a walking boot in your life and are thinking of bagging a *levada*, the following is essential kit: sturdy walking boots, walking poles, mobile phone, a good map and walking guide, a water bottle, food and emergency rations, waterproofs, a windproof jacket, a hiker's first aid kit, a torch, sun block, hat and whistle.

Shopping

Madeira offers many tempting buys, from good quality handicrafts to food and drink. And with Portugal being one of the least expensive countries in the euro zone, you get more bang for your buck.

Madeira Mementos

Traditional handicrafts have survived on Madeira thanks to tourism. Cottage industries such as embroidery, tapestry, wickerwork and knitting all flourish under the watchful eye of IBTAM (▷ 33) , an organization that guarantees authenticity and administers certification. Other souvenirs of the island include orchids, *bolo de mel* (molasses cake), sugary liqueurs and Madeira's famous fortified wine—the most common item to weigh down suitcases on the plane home. There's no shortage of places to buy such items; stalls congregate wherever tourists do. With no hard sell or haggling, shopping is generally a pleasant experience. For a better class of souvenir, head for Patrício & Gouveia (▷ 42) or Casa do Turista (▷ 40), both in Funchal.

Retail Explosion

In recent years Madeirans have witnessed a retail boom, with huge malls springing up in and around Funchal. They have branches of international chains as well as cafés, restaurants and cinemas. Hopefully these shopping complexes will not kill off Funchal's quaint city-centre boutiques.

KNIT-PICKING

It may be the last thing you'd expect to bring home from a tropical island off Africa, but Madeiran knitwear, essential kit in the island's cool mountainous interior, is quite a hit among tourists. Chunky sweaters, socks, gloves and bright Andes-style bobble hats with ear flaps are the most popular items, and you'll see them stacked up in souvenir shops and on roadside stalls throughout the island. Madeiran knitwear isn't the last word in fashion, but it's warm and inexpensive.

Madeira wine from Blandy's and hand-embroidered table linen make great gifts or souvenirs

Madeira by Night

Although not known as a party city, Funchal provides many enjoyable ways to while away the evenings, with everything from British pubs, fashionable bars and characterful restaurants to thumping discos and the glitzy Casino da Madeira.

Late Night Options

Classy Madeira doesn't promote itself as a hedonist's heaven and those seeking all-you-can-drink bars and a raucous club scene should probably head for other islands. Madeira pitches its mild-mannered nightlife to an older generation, expats and families, though Funchal and Machico have one night-club each. The Casino da Madeira (▷ 43) provides weekend fun with a dinner-and-show combo, and several British and Irish pubs have live music and imported beers. A touch of local spice is provided by Arsenios (▷ 45) in the Zona Velha where traditional Portuguese *fado* music is performed nightly. Classical music concerts, events at the English Church (▷ 43), occasional theatre performances and local festivals add to the mix of entertainment.

Beyond the Capital

Outside the Funchal area, nightlife options are extremely limited, with restaurants and the odd bar providing some degree of diversion. But annual festivals bring rural communities to life, and special events are occasionally held at cultural venues and galleries. Hotel restaurants sometimes lay on live music.

Nightlife centres on Funchal, where there are cool bars, live fado and a small club scene

---

CARNIVAL!

Without doubt, Funchal's liveliest time of the year is carnival night in mid-February. Rio it may not be, but Funchal's energetic procession, which sambas its way from the seafront to Praça do Município, is a much more intimate affair. Crowds line the specially illuminated streets as elaborately decorated floats cruise past and dancers gyrate to Latin rhythms. Madeirans really let their hair down in a rare display of exuberance.

Eating Out

Stick to dishes made with produce harvested from the Atlantic, grown in the island's volcanic soil and reared on the high pastures of the interior's Paúl da Serra, and you will experience the essence of Madeiran cooking.

Where, When, How?

Funchal has a wide choice of places to eat, from breakfast cafés and low-cost lunch spots to fine dining and traditional taverns with musical entertainment. Opening times vary from place to place but almost all establishments open for lunch and dinner. Dress is smart casual at all but the most exclusive places; service is normally prompt and tips are welcome.

Mainstays of the Madeiran Menu

Traditional Madeiran menus feature plenty of fish, especially *espada* (scabbard), which comes in up to 15 different guises. Some say the quintessential Madeiran main is *espada com banana*—Atlantic-caught scabbard with fried banana. *Espada* should not to be confused with *espetada*, barbecued beef on a laurel spit. Other Madeiran classics include *caldeirada* (fish stew), *feijoada* (bean casserole) and *milho frito* (fried polenta). Be aware that most shellfish are air-freighted onto the island and not locally caught. Pudding often revolves around an uninspiring choice of fruit and ice cream; instead plump for addictive *bolo de mel* (molasses cake) or the ubiquitous *pastel de nata* (custard tart).

A DROP TO DRINK

Some tourists automatically order Madeira wine with their meal, but no Madeiran ever would, as Madeira is a fortified dessert wine. Instead, order a light Portuguese white or rosé. Despite the strong British presence on the island, tea is frequently a disappointment—just a tea bag in a cup of lukewarm water. However, coffee is superb and juices often freshly squeezed. Tap water, while perfectly potable, leaves a rather volcanic aftertaste.

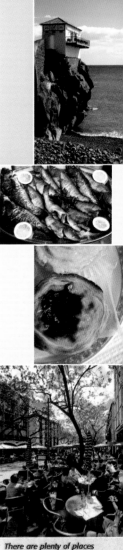

There are plenty of places to find good food, whether you fancy a fish platter or a delectable pastel de nata

Restaurants by Cuisine

There are restaurants, cafés and bars to suit all tastes and budgets on Madeira. On this page they are listed by cuisine. For a more detailed description of each restaurant, see Madeira by Area.

FINE DINING

Dona Amélia (▷ 46)
Il Gallo d'Oro (▷ 46)
Quinta do Monte (▷ 62)
Quinta Palmeira (▷ 48)
Villa Cipriani (▷ 48)

LIGHT BITES

Adega A Cuba (▷ 45)
Alto Monte (▷ 62)
Café do Museu (▷ 45)
Café de Parque (▷ 62)
Café República (▷ 62)
Café do Teatro (▷ 45)
Casa de Chá (▷ 106)
Espiga (▷ 78)
Ferro Velho (▷ 78)
Herédia (▷ 92)
Leque (▷ 47)
Penha D'Aguia (▷ 47)
Reid's Tea Terrace (▷ 48)
Sol Poente (▷ 92)
Vale das Freiras (▷ 62)

MADEIRAN/ PORTUGUESE

Arsenios (▷ 45)
A Bica (▷ 45)
Casa Madeirense (▷ 46)
Casa Velha (▷ 46)
Churrascaria Santana
  (▷ 78)
Cidade Velha (▷ 46)
Estrela do Norte (▷ 78)
Faisca (▷ 78)
Fim do Século (▷ 46)
Gavião Novo (▷ 46)
O Jango (▷ 47)
Lareira Portuguesa (▷ 47)
Mar á Vista (▷ 92)
Mercado Velho (▷ 106)
O Pescador, Machico
  (▷ 106)
O Pescador, Santana
  (▷ 78)
O Portão (▷ 47)
O Regional (▷ 48)
O Relógio (▷ 106)

Rocha Mar (▷ 92)
São Pedro (▷ 48)
O Tapassol (▷ 48)
Tokos (▷ 48)
Vila Baleia (▷ 92)
Vila do Peixe (▷ 62)
O Virgílio (▷ 78)

INTERNATIONAL

Apolo (▷ 45)
Armazém do Sal (▷ 45)
Beatles Boat (▷ 45)
Beerhouse (▷ 45)
Borda D'Agua (▷ 92)
A Brisa do Mar (▷ 106)
Cabrestante (▷ 106)
Cachalote (▷ 92)
Cantinho dos Mariscos
  (▷ 62)
Cantinho da Serra
  (▷ 78)
Casa Itália (▷ 45)
Churchill (▷ 62)
Dom Luis (▷ 92)
É Prá Picanha (▷ 46)
O Galã (▷ 106)
Gonçalves (▷ 106)
Grand Café Golden Gate
  (▷ 46)
Momentos Gourmet
  (▷ 47)
A Muralha (▷ 47)
Olives (▷ 47)
Onda Azul (▷ 92)
Qasbah (▷ 47)
Riso (▷ 48)
Taj Mahal (▷ 48)

If You Like...

However you'd like to spend your time on Madeira, these ideas should help you plan the perfect visit. Each suggestion has been cross-referenced to the fuller write-up elsewhere in the book.

SHOPPING FOR CRAFTS

Push through the crowds to the multicoloured stalls at Funchal's Mercado dos Lavradores. The craft outlets—wickerwork and leather—are on the ground floor (▷ 27).

Lose yourself in the souvenir-laden halls of the Casa do Turista (▷ 40).

Browse beautiful pieces of traditional needle-work at Bordal (▷ 40).

PARTYING UNTIL THE EARLY HOURS

Make merry as Madeira sleeps at Funchal's Vespas nightclub (▷ 44).

Place your bets at Madeira's Casino (▷ 43), where you can also enjoy dinner and a show.

Bop till you drop at Machico's La Barca disco (▷ 105).

Rustic hand-knits (top); bright lights beckon at the Casino (above); Choupana Hills (below)

HOT HOTELS

Check out the sleek designer decor and sumptuous roof-top pool at The Vine Hotel (▷ 111).

Feel the funky vibes at Funchal Design Hotel (▷ 110).

Chill out at Funchal's Choupana Hills (▷ 112), considered one of Europe's finest resort hotels.

Climbing aboard a toboggan in Monte (below)

COOL TRIPS

Look down upon the rooftops and gardens of Funchal from the Funchal–Monte cable car (▷ 61).

Jump aboard a traditional toboggan (▷ 59) on an exhilarating journey from Monte to Livramento.

Perfect your hill starts on a roller coaster tour of the island (▷ 77).

Dolphin-spotting

WILDLIFE

View life below the Atlantic Ocean aboard the glass-bottomed *Beluga* Submarine (▷ 43).

Spot dolphins and whales aboard the *Bonita da Madeira* (▷ 43).

Cruise to the Desertas Islands on the *Gavião* yacht (▷ 43) and see dolphins, seals, turtles, seabirds and other wildllife.

FABULOUS FOOD

Tuck into first-rate fare at Dona Amélia in Funchal (▷ 46).

Savour the genuine Zona Velha (Old Quarter) experience at Gavião Novo (▷ 46).

Bag a table at Funchal's stylish O Tapassol (▷ 48), popular among Madeira connoisseurs.

Step back in time over afternoon tea on Reid's Tea Terrace (▷ 48).

Reid's Tea Terrace (above)

GORGEOUS GARDENS

Wander through the understated beauty of Palheiro Gardens (▷ 60).

Lose yourself in the tropical Monte Palace Gardens (▷ 58).

Ogle the blooms in the Botanical Gardens (▷ 56).

The elegant Palheiro Gardens (above)

BEACH FUN

Catch some rays on the beach on Porto Santo (▷ 37), the archipelago's only naturally sandy shoreline.

Try out Machico's new public beach (▷ 100).

Choose between two sandy beaches at Calheta (▷ 82).

Golden sands, Porto Santo

GETTING OUT MORE

Blaze a spectacular peak-to-peak trail from Pico do Arieiro to the top of Pico Ruivo (▷ 68), Madeira's highest mountain.

Soak up the grandeur of the Boca da Encumeada (below)

Pull on your boots for a high-altitude hike from Boca da Encumeada to Pico Ruivo (▷ 66).

Go with the flow alongside one of the island's many *levada* aqueducts (▷ 67).

TAKING THE KIDS

Romp through Madeira-in-miniature at the Madeira Theme Park (▷ 74).

Enjoy a hands-on experience at Porto Moniz's Living Science Centre (▷ 83).

Wield bucket and spade on the sandy shores of Madeira's sister island, Porto Santo (▷ 37).

QUINTA ESSENTIAL

Rummage through Madeira's most intriguing museum, housed in the grand Quinta das Cruzes on the edge of Funchal (▷ 30).

Family fun at the Madeira Theme Park (above); inside historic Quinta das Cruzes, (below)

Dine in style at the elegant Quinta do Monte (▷ 112).

Sleep it off at the wonderful Quinta Splendida, a spa-resort in Caniço, east of Funchal (▷ 112).

POINTS OF VIEW

Climb up Pico dos Barcelos for sweeping vistas across Funchal (▷ 55).

Peer down on Curral das Freiras from Eira do Serrado viewing point (▷ 55) in southern Madeira.

Get two views for the price of one at Boca da Encumeada mountain pass where both the north and south coasts are visible (▷ 66).

Walk out onto 'Madeira's balcony' at the Balcões viewing point (▷ 71), an easy walk from Ribeiro Frio.

Dramatic valley view: Curral das Freiras (above right)

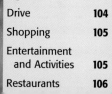

The capital of Madeira, with over 100,000 inhabitants, Funchal is built in a natural amphitheatre. Its sun-kissed basalt and marble streets, with hazy Atlantic vistas at every turn, are filled with people, yellow buses and taxis.

101

233

Museu
Photographia
Vicentes
Quinta das Cruzes
Convento de Santa Clara
Casa Museu Frederico de Freitas
Museu Municipal
Adegas de São Francisco
Sé

São
Martinho

261
Ponta da Cruz
▲

Cais da Cidade

Casa Branca

Piornais

Ponta da Cruz   *Ponta Gorda*

FUNCHAL

Bom Sucesso

Museu Henrique e Francisco Franco

Museu
de Arte
Sacra

IBTAM

Mercado dos Lavradores

Zona Velha

Madeira Story Centre

Museu
A Cidade
do Açúcar

São Gonçalo

Fortaleza de
São Tiago

0   2 km
0   1 mile

Ⓗ

Casa Museu
Frederico de Freitas

HIGHLIGHTS

● The mansion's secluded winter garden, accessible from several rooms
● Stunning collection of ceramic tiles from the Middle East, North Africa and Europe

TIP

● Check out the temporary art exhibitions, featuring local and international artists, staged in a hall next to the main house.

Packed with exquisite objets d'art and curios from around the world, the house-museum of Frederico de Freitas provides a fascinating glimpse of the life of a 20th-century collector and colourful Madeiran character.

All in good taste Built by the counts of Calçada in the mid-17th century, this fine mansion was purchased by Frederico de Freitas, a well-connected Funchal lawyer, in the 1940s. Over the next three decades Freitas filled it with art, furniture, carpets and antiques acquired on his many travels around the world. The joy of visiting the high-ceilinged mansion is in wandering the beautifully furnished rooms, each one a temple to Freitas's exquisite taste. Freitas was a compulsive collector of jugs and cups; a tiny

The elegant interior and stunning winter garden of the Casa Museu Frederico de Freitas capture the character of its owner, an aesthete and avid collector; his home makes a fitting setting for the Casa dos Azulejos, devoted to the lovely glazed tiles that are a feature of the Iberian peninsula and North Africa

fraction of 2,000 such items, ranging from the finest Wedgwood to souvenir mugs produced for London's Chelsea Football Club, are displayed in a dedicated room.

Gorgeous ceramics Housed in an annex next to the mansion, the Casa dos Azulejos (Tile Museum) tells how the art of tile-making and glazing spread from the Middle East to northern Europe via North Africa and the Iberian Peninsula. There are tile fragments from ancient Persia, wonderful geometric designs from Tunisia, ceramics from England and Holland, as well as typical Madeiran *azulejos*, the brightly coloured tiles used to decorate the walls, steeples and altarpieces of the island's churches, including early examples from the nearby Convento de Santa Clara (▷ 33).

THE BASICS

🕂 a1
✉ Calçada de Santa Clara 7
☎ 91 202 570
🕐 Tue–Sat 10–5.30
♿ Good
👜 Inexpensive

Adegas de São Francisco

Tools of the trade in the Adegas de São Francisco: a wine press and barrels of maturing Verdelho

TOP 25

FUNCHAL

THE BASICS

- b2
- Avenida Arriaga 28
- 291 740 110
- Mon–Fri 10–6.30, Sat 10–1. Guided tours Mon–Fri 10.30, 2.30, 3.30 and 4.30, Sat 11
- Few
- Moderate (for tours)

HIGHLIGHT

- Post-tour tasting session where you can sample the four big hitters of the Madeira wine world—Sercial Bual, Verdelho and Malmsey

TIP

- If you can't make up your mind which Madeira is for you, leave the decision until the airport where the Old Blandy's shop (after security) offers a last chance to buy.

Funchal's oldest wine lodge, Adegas de São Francisco is an atmospheric place where the air is heavy with both a sense of history and the sweet aroma of Madeira's celebrated tipple.

Holy origins Known to many as Old Blandy's Wine Lodge, the former Monastery of St Francis became a wine store in 1834. Its 17th-century beams and wisteria-wreathed balconies provide an attractive setting for the ageing, tasting and sale of Madeira's famous fortified wine. Huge American oak and Brazilian satinwood barrels contain wine by the big names of the Madeiran wine market—Blandy's, Leacock's, Cossart Gordan and Miles. These British merchant families came to dominate the island's wine exports when Britain was granted special trading rights with Madeira in the 17th century.

Tour and taste You can wander through the various shops and tasting rooms on your own, but taking the hour-long guided tour brings the industry to life. Knowledgeable guides explain the traditional wine-producing process step by step, from the vine to 150-year-old bottles lying on dusty shelves, the wine inside still maturing. No visit to a winery is complete without a tasting session, and the tour ends in the bar, where you get to 'sip history', as Winston Churchill described the experience of drinking Madeira. After the tour, the vintage room is your chance to buy wines dating back to the 19th century—just alert your bank beforehand.

TOP 25

The curvy exterior of the Mercado dos Lavradores (left); a fine display of island produce (right)

TOP 25

Mercado dos Lavradores

Brimming with cut flowers, fish and fruit, Funchal's central market blazes with tropical colour and hums with the hubbub of traders, shoppers and tourists.

Madeira's fruit basket Built in the 1930s by Edmundo Tavares, one of Portugal's best known modern architects, the 'Workers' Market' is an impressive building built around an inner courtyard where the daily (except Sunday) fruit and veg market takes place. Stalls weighed down with every kind of produce, including many you won't recognize, line the upper level of the market, while wicker shops and souvenir emporiums fill the halls around the courtyard. Throughout the market are panels of *azulejos* (glazed tiles), some depicting harvests and market scenes, others forming geometric patterns in ultramarine, white and ochre.

Something fishy The most animated area of the market in the early morning is the fish hall, where you'll see Funchal's chefs and restaurant owners buying up scabbard, tuna and sardines, while locals snap up herring, mullet and bream.

National symbols You can't miss the flower sellers, who congregate just inside the entrance to the market. Dressed in Madeira's traditional folk costume—striped skirt, red bodice and white blouse—they are almost as colourful as the exotic flowers they sell. The orange 'birds of paradise' (strelitzia), Madeira's national flower, are particularly spectacular.

THE BASICS

- d2
- Largo dos Lavradores
- Mon–Thu 7–4, Fri 7–8, Sat 7–5
- Restaurants and cafés in and around the market
- None
- Free

HIGHLIGHTS

- The flower sellers in traditional costume who congregate near the entrance
- The fish market, at its most animated before 10am

TIPS

- Avoid buying from fruit sellers who offer lots of free samples—they charge extortionate prices.
- Support Madeiran businesses by buying only local produce and goods.

Museu de Arte Sacra

TOP
25

Housed in the former Bishop's Palace, this museum's collection of priceless Flemish art was bought with proceeds from the trade in sugar—Madeira's home-grown treasure.

Holy silver The Bishop's Palace, built in 1600 and remodelled in the mid-18th century, is worth seeing in its own right. Its high ceilings, creaky hardwood floors, basalt-framed windows and doors and pebble-dash courtyard form a handsome setting for a splendid collection. The first floor displays18th- and 19th-century church silverware and sculptures in wood, including an almost life-sized Last Supper, and pieces from the Indo-Portuguese School. Many exhibits were brought here from churches around the island, including several artefacts from the Sé.

The former Bishop's Palace contains an outstanding collection of Flemish paintings, including the Machico Adoration (right), peopled by wealthy Madeiran landowners and sugar merchants of the time, who commissioned the Flemish artists

Master strokes The pride of the museum is the collection of Flemish masters displayed on the top floor. Between the 16th and 18th centuries Madeiran merchants, flush with profits from the sugar trade, commissioned top Flemish artists to produce paintings for *quintas* and churches across the island (transferred here for safe-keeping in the 1950s). Ships sailed to Antwerp laden with sugar and returned to Funchal bearing cargoes of art. The large dimensions of the oak panel paintings and altarpieces hint at the immense wealth of the merchants. Highlights in the museum's collection include works by Pieter Coecke van Aelst (1502–50), Joost van Cleve (died 1540) and Gerard David (1468–1523), whose triptych *Descent from the Cross* is particularly dramatic and moving.

THE BASICS

www.museuartesacra
funchal.org

✚ b2
✉ Rua do Bispo 21
☎ 291 228 900
🕐 Tue–Sat 10–12.30, 2.30–6.30, Sun 10–1
🍴 Café do Museu (€)
♿ None
💷 Inexpensive

Quinta das Cruzes

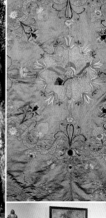

HIGHLIGHTS

● The *quinta's* dazzling silverware and the exhibition of furniture made out of sugar cases
● Water features in the gardens of the museum

TIP

● The grounds can be visited free of charge, even during the long lunch break.

Brimming with period furniture and precious works of art, the 'Mansion of the Crosses' is perhaps the island's most engaging museum.

Gracious living This *quinta* is the only one on the island that has opened its doors to the paying public. Commissioned in the 18th century by a wealthy family of Genoese wine merchants, it is built on the site of a house that belonged to Zarco, the 15th-century discoverer of Madeira and its first governor. Before visiting the main house, explore the grounds, a delightful oasis with rounded pebble steps, splashing water features and an alfresco exhibition of tombstones and decorative fragments salvaged from old Funchal buildings, including, it is claimed, masonry from Zarco's residence. The grounds

Clockwise from far left: carved window detail in the garden of the Quinta das Cruzes; lustrous silk wall hangings; ivy-clad stonework; the imposing 18th-century facade; some of the Brazilian satinwood furniture made from old sugar chests

are peppered with benches in the shade of mature trees, ideal spots for a picnic lunch if you are waiting for the museum to reopen after its midday break.

Grand interior Inside, exhibits are arranged thematically. In addition to fine period furniture, jewellery, oil paintings and porcelain, there are intricately carved gemstones, a watch that belonged to Emperor Charles I, examples of 18th- and 19th-century transport on Madeira, silverware and *caixa de açucar*—utilitarian furniture fashioned from Brazilian satinwood packing cases. Sugar was shipped from Madeira in boxes made of this wood, but when the trade eventually dried up, enterprising carpenters recycled the leftover material to fashion chunky cabinets, tables and chests of drawers.

Sé

The cathedral's distinctive tiled spire (left) and its striking choir stalls (right)

THE BASICS

- ✚ C2
- ✉ Largo da Sé
- ☎ 291 228 155
- 🕐 Daily 9–12.30, 4–5.30
- ♿ Good
- 🎫 Free

HIGHLIGHTS

- Manueline architectural elements, including the *azulejos*-decorated spire
- The cathedral's intricately carved ceiling made from indigenous cedar

TIP

- Services at the Sé are held at 8am, 8.30am, 11.15am and 6pm.

Madeira's Gothic cathedral has dominated Funchal's cityscape for five centuries and is essential viewing for any visitor.

Royal funding Decorative elements punctuate the Sé's rather stern basalt and whitewash exterior. The chequered *azulejos* on the spire are a typical feature of Madeiran churches (some of the original tiles are displayed at the Casa Museu Frederico de Freitas); the turrets, resembling twists of barley sugar, are characteristic of the Manueline period, when King Manuel I of Portugal (1495–1521) funded the construction of churches and other public buildings, including the Sé. Below the modest rose window, the portal bears King Manuel I's coat of arms, incorporating the red cross of the Knights Templar. King Manuel was the grand master of this military order and its cross often featured on Manueline buildings and on the sails of Portuguese ships of the day.

The interior The cathedral's gloomy interior is aromatic with the musty fragrance of candle wax. Look up to see the impressive ceiling carved in local cedar and inlaid with ivory, its geometric designs clearly influenced by Moorish Spain. Take a pew to appreciate the beautifully carved choir stalls; resplendent with near life-size figures of the Apostles depicted in gold on a blue background, they were carved in Flanders and financed by Madeira's money-spinning sugar trade. The large baroque gilt altar was added in the 18th century.

More to See

CONVENTO DE SANTA CLARA

Funchal's 15th-century convent is home to around 25 nuns, who gladly welcome visitors to their tranquil city centre retreat. The high point of the guided tour is the Church of Our Lady, resplendent in *azulejos*. The church is also the final resting place of Zarco, who claimed the island for Portugal in 1420 and became its first governor.

🚼 a1 ✉ Calçada de Santa Clara ☎ 291 742 602 🕓 Mon–Sat 10–12, 3–5 💷 Inexpensive

FORTALEZA DE SÃO TIAGO

www.museumac.com

Built in the early 17th century to defend Funchal from pirate attacks, this ochre-coloured fortress housed British troops during the Napoleonic Wars; afterwards many stayed on and made the island their home. The Portuguese Army was stationed here until 1992, when the fort was refashioned as a museum of Portuguese contemporary art from the1960s to the present day. One

section of the museum is dedicated to Madeiran artists of the 1980s and '90s, and temporary exhibitions occupy a special gallery.

🚼 e3 ✉ Rua do Portão de São Tiago ☎ 291 213 340 🕓 Mon–Sat 10–12.30, 2–5.30 🍴 Numerous restaurants in the nearby Zona Velha 💷 Inexpensive

IBTAM

IBTAM (Instituto do Bordado, Tapeçarias e Artesanato da Madeira) is the body that promotes, regulates and oversees traditional handicrafts on Madeira, in particular embroidery and tapestry. The organization's hologram, attached to everything from handkerchiefs to bedspreads, serves as a guarantee that an item has been made by hand on the island. The quaint museum at the institute's headquarters focuses on embroidery, with mock-ups of 19th-century living quarters bedecked in exquisitely embroidered textiles. One room traces the history of Madeiran embroidery, and the self-guided

Embroidery at IBTAM

The 15th-century Convento de Santa Clara

tour ends with a film on traditional island industries, IBTAM's work and the certification of Madeiran handicrafts. Hanging above the staircase leading up to the museum is a tapestry depicting the natural abundance of the Madeiran landscape. This mammoth work took three years to complete and is said to contain over seven million stitches.

➕ d1 ✉ Rua Visconde do Anadia 44 ☎ 291 211 600 🕐 Mon–Fri 9.30–12.30, 2–5.30 💶 Inexpensive

MADEIRA STORY CENTRE (MSC)

www.storycentre.com

If you like your history fired up with multimedia technology, the MSC is for you. Touch screen games, smell boxes and hands-on artefacts, as well as more traditional museum exhibits such as early maps and astrolabes and a working model of a sugar mill, flesh out the island's history from its volcanic beginnings to the modern day. For a lively overview of Madeira's past, and the characters who have shaped its

destiny, there's no better museum, and the interactive features make it an attention-grabbing half-day's entertainment for children.

➕ d2 ✉ Rua D. Carlos I 27–29 ☎ 291 000 770 🕐 Daily 10–6 ♿ Good 💶 Expensive

MUSEU A CIDADE DO AÇUCAR

Funchal's Sugar Museum is built around the excavated remains of a house where Christopher Columbus stayed after his voyage to the Americas in 1498. It traces the history of sugar production on Madeira and its trade in northern Europe; among the exhibits are sugar cones similar to those depicted on Funchal's coat of arms, and religious art commissioned by the island's wealthy merchants.

➕ c2 ✉ Praça de Colombo 5 ☎ 291 236 910 🕐 Mon–Fri 10–12.30, 2–6 💶 Inexpensive

MUSEU HENRIQUE E FRANCISCO FRANCO

Though off the beaten tourist trail, this is an interesting museum

Hands-on exhibits at the Madeira Story Centre

showcasing the work of two artist brothers born and raised on Madeira—sculptor Francisco Franco (1855–1955) and Henrique Franco (1883–1961), a painter. As students studying in Paris, the brothers found themselves rubbing shoulders with Picasso and Degas; later on, they moved to Lisbon, where they produced many of their best works. The museum displays drawings, sculptures and paintings.

➕ d1 ✉ Rua de João de Deus 13 ☎ 291 230 633 🕓 Mon–Fri 10–12.30, 2–6 💷 Inexpensive

MUSEU MUNICIPAL

Funchal's Municipal Museum, focusing entirely on the island's natural history, is probably the city's least visited attraction. It includes a modest aquarium containing many of the species of fish found in the waters around the archipelago, such as miserable-looking grouper fish, wild-eyed moray eels and bottom-dwelling flounders. Climb the stairs to view the well-tended taxidermy collection, including sharks, giant crabs and many of the island's bird species.

➕ a1 ✉ Rua da Mouraria 31 ☎ 291 225 050 🕓 Tue–Fri 10–6, Sat–Sun 12–6 💷 Inexpensive

MUSEU PHOTOGRAPHIA VICENTES

www.museumac.com

This photographic studio established by Vicente Gomes da Silva in 1865 looks almost exactly as it did when Vicente was processing his snapshots of famous visitors to the island in the19th century. Originally built in the garden of a Funchal townhouse, it served as a studio to four generations of the Gomes da Silva family until it was preserved as a museum in 1982. Inside, there's a dark room, displays of ancient and not-so-old cameras and some of the fanciful backdrops that studio photography employed, reminding modern-day digital photographers of how much effort and skill once went into creating

Detail of Funchal's coat of arms depicted in tiles at the Museu a Cidade do Açucar

Painting in the Museu Franco

quality images. The museum also possesses a stock of 800,000 negatives documenting life on the island in the late 19th and most of the 20th century. Beneath the old-fashioned Vicentes sign, the shady courtyard has a pleasant café.

⊞ b2 ✉ Rua da Carreira 43 ☎ 291 225 050 🕓 Mon–Fri 10–12.30, 2–5 🍴 Café (€) 📋 Inexpensive

ZONA VELHA (OLD QUARTER)

Wedged between the Praça da Autonomia and the São Tiago Fort, this area of narrow cobbled lanes lined with old fishermen's houses, some dating back to the days of the first settlers, is Funchal's most characterful quarter. By day the shady streets are great for aimless wandering; at night the highest concentration of restaurants in any part of Funchal makes it a mecca for the hungry, especially those in search of traditional Madeiran dishes or seafood. Despite this, the Zona Velha is still very much a place where people live, shop and dry their washing across narrow alley-ways, and it is still decades away from gentrification. Above it all, glid-ing incongruously over the rooftops, are the cable cars of the *teleféricos* (▷ 61), their tourist passengers peering down into once hidden corners of old Funchal.

The focal point of the Old Quarter is the Largo do Corpo Santo, an elongated square occupied by numerous eateries and the diminu-tive Capela do Corpo Santo, a fishermen's chapel dating from the 16th century and one of the oldest churches on the island. Another notable church in the Zona Velha is the Igreja de Santa Maria Maior in Rua de Santa Maria. Sometimes known as the Igreja de São Tiago, this chunk of baroque architecture was erected in memory of plague victims in the 16th century and remodelled in the 18th century; it has one of Madeira's most attractive baroque interiors.

⊞ e2 🍴 Numerous restaurants and cafés ♿ Few

Zona Velha is the hub of Funchal's restaurant scene

EXCURSION TO PORTO SANTO

Some 40km (25 miles) to the northeast of Madeira is the tiny island of Porto Santo. Its long stretches of sun-drenched beach, undeveloped coastline and mostly treeless interior are in stark contrast to the tropical greenery, mountain vistas and rocky basalt coasts of the main island. But if you've had your fill of climbing steep hills and tanning on concrete beaches, Porto Santo provides a pleasant change. Even the weather is more predictable, with warmer temperatures and very little rainfall even in winter, attracting foreign tourists year-round and thousands of Portuguese in the summer months.

The island's only town is Vila Baleira, lying just back from the beach and a 10-minute drive from the airport. Top billing in this peaceful, whitewashed community goes to the Casa Museu Cristóvão Colombo (Christopher Columbus Museum House; Travessa da Sacristia, tel 291 983 405) where Columbus, a sugar trader before he became an explorer, lived after marrying the daughter of the island's governor in the late 1470s.

From Vila Baleira, it takes literally minutes to reach the other attractions on the island, including an 18-hole, par 72 golf course (tel 291 983 778), designed by Seve Ballesteros, and the Fonte da Areia (Fountain of the Sands), a natural health-giving spring where you can sample the water. The best way to explore the island is to hire a bike or scooter in Vila Baleira and zip around at your own convenience. For more information on travel options between Madeira and Porto Santo (▷ 117). Ferry timetables on most (but not all) days make an extended day-trip from Funchal possible; the crossing takes around two hours and 15 minutes.

➕ *B11* 🛈 Avenida Henrique Vieira e Castro, tel 291 982 361 🍴 Restaurants in Vila Baleira 🛫 Porto Santo Airport, tel 291 980 120; www.anam.pt ⛴ Porto Santo Line, 291 210 300; www.portosantoline.pt ♿ Few

The long golden sands of Porto Santo

Walk around Funchal Centre

Take a stroll through the city centre and discover Funchal's rich architectural heritage.

DISTANCE: 1km (0.5 miles) **ALLOW:** 30 minutes

START

CÂMARA MUNICIPAL (TOWN HALL) ✚ c1

1 Begin the walk with a quick peek into the palm-filled courtyard of the elegant Câmara Municipal (Town Hall), built by the Count of Carvalhal in the 18th century. In the centre of the courtyard is a sculpture of Leda and the Swan (1880).

2 From the Town Hall, cross the basalt- and marble-paved Praça do Município to the Igreja do Colégio, built by the Jesuits in 1629. Across the square is the Bishop's Palace, home to the Museu de Arte Sacra (Sacred Art Museum) (▷ 28).

3 With your back to the church, turn right into Rua C. Pestana, which becomes Rua da Carreira at the junction with Avenida Zarco. Keep going straight on.

END

CEMITÉRIO INGLÊS (BRITISH CEMETERY) ✚ a1

7 Keep going up Rua Quebra Costas to the Cemitério Inglês (British Cemetery), packed with 19th-century tombstones. All of Madeira's Protestants are buried here regardless of nationality.

6 The third street on the right is the Rua Quebra Costas, which leads to the neoclassical English Church, a frequent venue for concerts (▷ 43).

5 Continue up Rua da Carreira, dipping in and out of its little shops. Look up to see the wrought-iron balconies protruding from the upper floors. House No. 155 has a fine example.

4 Three doors up on the left, turn into a courtyard belonging to the Museu Photographia Vicentes (▷ 35), with its sweeping staircase and nicely shaded café.

WALK

FUNCHAL

Walk Around
Funchal's Harbour

Time this waterside amble right, and you can finish just in time to admire the short-lived Atlantic sunset from a pavement café.

DISTANCE: 1.5km (1 mile) **ALLOW:** 1 hour

START

THE TOURIST OFFICE
🔳 b2

① Kick off at the tourist office in Avenida Arriaga. Facing the building, turn to the left. After a few steps you'll arrive at the lush Municipal Gardens, an ideal picnic spot.

② A few more paces along Avenida Arriaga bring you to the Adegas de São Francisco (▷ 26). Cross the street to admire the Toyota showroom adorned with some exquisite *azulejos* panels. Next door is the Baltazar Dias Municipal Theatre, built in1888.

③ Take the street beyond the theatre (Rua do Conselheiro José Silvestre Ribeiro) and head downhill towards the seafront. At the bottom is the entrance to the amazing Casa do Turista (▷ 40).

END

**LARGO DA SE
(CATHEDRAL SQUARE)** 🔳 c2

⑦ Head up the street just before the parliament towards the Largo da Sé (Cathedral Square) with its cafés.

⑥ Keep going along Avenida do Mar. On the left is the Madeiran Regional Parliament with its circular debating chamber. On the right stands the stump of the Banger's Tower, the remnants of an 18th-century crane.

⑤ You are now on Avenida do Mar. The 16th-century Palácio de São Lourenço bristles with cannon to the left while the marina is filled with masts and sails to your right.

④ Turn right if you fancy a walk along the Molhe da Pontinha, the massive sea wall. It's a great place to get panoramic snaps of Funchal. Otherwise turn left.

Shopping

AGENCIA DE LEILÕES SÃO PEDRO

This small antiques shop sells beautiful clocks, jugs, lamps and ceramics. Erratic opening times.
➕ b2 ✉ Rua das Pretas 69–73

AIRES & FILHOSO

An enchanting antiques shop stocking heaps of traditional ceramics, clocks, silverware, paintings, dark wood furniture and curios under the beams and arches of an old Funchal townhouse.
➕ a2 ✉ Rua da Mouraria 36 ☎ 291 235 387

ARTECOURO

This city centre leather shop sells a small selection of locally made items. You might be able to arrange a visit to their workshop near the Botanical Gardens (Rua Carlos Azevedo Menezes 18) if you call the shop in advance.
➕ b2 ✉ Rua da Alfândega 15 ☎ 291 237 256

BAZAR DO POVO

In business since the 1880s, this department store claims to be Funchal's longest established shop. It has a book department selling maps and guides to the island, and there is a café.
➕ b1 ✉ Rua do Bettencourt ☎ 291 202 560

BOA VISTA ORCHIDS

Founded in the 1960s by a British orchid fanatic, this is one of the best places on the island for fantastic blooms and worth the trip even if you don't want to buy. It is located in the subtropical gardens of the Quinta da Boa Vista to the northeast of the Mercado dos Lavradores.
➕ G8 ✉ Rua Lombo da Boa Vista ☎ 291 220 468 🚌 32

BORDAL

www.bordal.pt
Bordal are official producers of embroidered cotton and linen, and this emporium and workshop are among the best places to view and buy embroidered tablecloths, bedspreads, towels and baby clothes. There are other branches at Avenida do Infante 26B, in the Dolce Vita shopping mall and at the airports.

SHOP OR MUSEUM?

Funchal's Casa do Turista is half-shop, half-tourist attraction; on entering you may feel you've wandered into the house-museum of a famous local of yore. Tables are beautifully laid with crystal and Portuguese ceramics, antique dressers are draped with embroidery, and crystal chandeliers hang from ornate stucco ceilings. Out back is a mock-up of a traditional thatched cottage where you may be offered a glass of Madeira to relax your grip on those euros.

➕ C2 ✉ Rua Dr. Fernão Ornelas 77 ☎ 291 222 965

O BORDÃO

If you've arrived without your hiking boots or waterproofs and want to head off into the wilds, this well-stocked outdoor shop is the place to get kitted out.
➕ b2 ✉ Rua da Carreira 173 ☎ 291 281 265

CASA

This is southern Europe's answer to IKEA: quirky contemporary design, heaps of fragrant candles and interestingly crafted household items.
➕ c2 ✉ Rua Dr. Fernão de Ornelas 56A and B ☎ 291 220 750

CASA DO TURISTA

The place to shop for souvenirs in Funchal, Casa do Turista is crammed with Madeira's best products. Just browsing around the place is an enjoyable way of spending an hour or so (▷ panel, left).
➕ c2 ✉ Rua do Conselheiro José Silvestre Ribeiro 2 ☎ 291 224 907

DIOGOS WINE SHOP

This long-established shop is one of the best wine outlets in Funchal, with free tastings, a basement museum dedicated to Christopher Columbus and a huge selection of Madeira wines. Staff are very knowledgeable about the wine they sell, and all

but the most expensive vintages can be sampled before purchase.
🔲 a2 ⊠ Avenida Arriaga 28 ☎ 291 233 357

DOLCE VITA

This gleaming new shopping mall just off the Rotunda do Infante has 58 shops (a blend of international and Portuguese chains), a large food court and ample subterranean parking. Hopefully, it won't drive the small city-centre shops out of business.
🔲 a2 ⊠ Rua Dr. Brito Câmaro 9 ☎ 291 215 420

D'OLIVEIRAS

The pervading musty-sweet aroma of Madeira wine, and dusty barrels piled up all around the store contribute to a captivating wine-purchasing experience in an historic setting. Generous free tastings.
🔲 b1 ⊠ Rua dos Ferreiros 107 ☎ 291 228 558

ELMA TAPESTRIES

This small boutique specializes in genuine hand-woven Madeiran tapestries, a dying art form on the island according to the owner. Pieces mostly depict scenes from traditional Madeiran life and the archipelago's native plants and animals.
🔲 G8 ⊠ Boutique 6, Savoy Hotel, Avenida do Infante ☎ 291 225 249 🚌 1, 2, 4, 6, 12

FÁBRICA SABORÁVEL

This age-old Funchal bakery, a five-minute walk north of Praça do Município, sells traditional biscuits, cakes and local spirits at non-tourist prices. It also serves the cheapest cup of coffee in town.
🔲 b1 ⊠ Rua dos Ferreiros 206 ☎ 291 222 565

FÁBRICA SANTO ANTONIO

This is a wonderful old-fashioned bakery where locals come to stock up on biscuits, *bolo de mel* (molasses cake), *pastéis de natal* (custard tarts) and various other sweet treats. It has been trading since 1893 and will doubtless still be around for years to come.
🔲 c2 ⊠ Travessa do Forno 27 ☎ 291 220 255

A STITCH UP

Embroidery was introduced to Madeira by Elizabeth Phelps, the daughter of an English wine merchant, as a means of supplementing local incomes following a cholera outbreak in the 1850s. Today, around 20,000 Madeirans are involved in this cottage industry, and embroidered tablecloths, napkins and clothes are popular buys among visitors. The embroidery is done by hand (genuine articles bear a hologram label) using traditional patterns.

FORUM MADEIRA

Handy if you are staying around the Lido or on the western end of the hotel zone, this modern mall has over 80 shops, a supermarket, cinemas, restaurants and a large car park. Retreat to the roof garden for Atlantic views and post-retail R&R.
🔲 G8 ⊠ Estrada Monumental 139 🚌 4, 48

GALERIAS SÃO LOURENÇO

This is slightly more upmarket and small-scale than Funchal's other shopping centres, with popular international chains sitting beside local boutiques, homeware stores and cafés.
🔲 B2 ⊠ Avenida Arriaga 41

GOODIES

If you're a Brit pining for some Patak's curry paste, Angel Delight or Twinings tea, this British minimart stocks them all and many other well-known brands.
🔲 G8 ⊠ Estrada Monumental 316, shop 1 ☎ 291 765 301 🚌 1, 2, 4, 6, 12

JARDIM ORQUÍDEA

Owned by the same family since 1905, this world of plants is as much retail experience as tourist attraction. There are some 50,000 plants on display, including hundreds of orchids (original and hybrid varieties) and many other types of tropical plants.

An admission charge applies.

🔲 G8 ✉ Rua Pita da Silva 37 ☎ 291 238 444 🚌 31

LIVRARIA ESPERANÇA

This bookshop is quaintly old-fashioned. It stocks maps and some English-language titles on *levada* walks. The main draw for locals lies over the road, at No. 156—the largest used bookstore in Portugal. Room after room in this grand old palace is packed to the rafters with all kinds of titles (in Portuguese).

🔲 b1 ✉ Rua dos Ferreiros 119 and 156 ☎ 291 221 116

LOJA DOS VINHOS

In the heart of the hotel zone, this wine and spirits shop is the place to come for a 1966 Bual or a 1979 Verdelho. There are barrels out front where you can sample different kinds of Madeira, with no obligation to buy.

🔲 G8 ✉ Estrada Monumental 314A ☎ 291 761 508 🚌 1, 2, 4, 6, 12

MADEIRA SHOPPING

To the west of the city, Madeira's largest shopping centre has over 100 outlets, selling many international brands and offering a seven-screen cinema, 1,000 parking places and even an exhibition on the *levadas*. It also has its own dedicated bus service from the city centre.

🔲 G8 ✉ Caminho de Santa Quitéria 45 ☎ 291 100 800 🚌 8

MADEIRA SUN

If you feel inspired by the local penchant for tapestry during your stay on Madeira, this popular arts and crafts shop sells a wide selection of DIY tapestry kits to take home.

🔲 b2 ✉ Avenida Zarco 4

MARINA SHOPPING

This multi-level emporium has international newsagents, a bookshop with maps and guides, and a supermarket. There are entrances on Avenida do Mar and Avenida Arriaga.

🔲 a3 ✉ Avenida Arriaga 75

MERCADO DOS LAVRADORES

As well as serving as a fruit, veg and fish market, Mercado dos Lavradores (▷ 27) sells leather

---

RETAIL EXPLOSION

Over the last decade Madeira has witnessed an explosion in the number of large shopping malls in both the city centre and out of town. These have been built to serve retail-hungry locals and the tens of thousands of tourists who descend on the island every year. Some fear these mega-malls may soon put the quaint old city-centre shops, some of them long-established family-run boutiques, out of business.

---

goods, wickerwork and wine, though prices here tend to be higher than in other souvenir hotspots.

🔲 d2 ✉ Largo dos Lavradores

OLD BLANDY'S WINE SHOP

Located at the entrance to the Adegas de São Francisco, Old Blandy's (▷ 26) is an institution. As well as selling Madeira's favourite tipple, it sells a good range of Portuguese wines, champagne, cigars and *bolo de mel* (molasses cake).

🔲 b2 ✉ Avenida Arriaga 28 ☎ 291 740 110

PATRÍCIO & GOUVEIA

Anyone seeking high quality souvenirs and handicrafts should head here. The ground floor is dedicated to top-notch embroidery produced in the workshop next door, while downstairs offers ceramics, brass and other handicrafts, as well as wine. Goods can be shipped to your home address for a price.

🔲 d1 ✉ Rua Visconde do Anadia 34 ☎ 291 220 801

RUA DR. FERNÃO ORNELAS

Like Spain, Portugal is well known for the quality of its footwear. This street is lined with shops selling boots, shoes and sandals for a fraction of the price you would pay at home.

🔲 c2 ✉ Rua Dr. Fernão Ornelas

Entertainment and Activities

BELUGA SUBMARINE
www.belugasubmarine.net
The two-and-a-half-hour sealife-watching trips aboard this glass-bottomed boat are highly recommended. Only sails in good weather.
🏠 b3 ✉ Marina do Funchal ☎ 967 044 217 🕔 Daily 11 and 3.30

BONITA DA MADEIRA
www.bonita-da-madeira.com
Go whale- and dolphin-spotting and cruising around the Desertas Islands aboard this 23m-long (75ft) sailboat.
🏠 b3 ✉ Marina do Funchal ☎ 291 762 218 🕔 Numerous daily sailings: check website for details

CASINO DA MADEIRA
Housed in one of Funchal's ugliest buildings, Madeira's casino (▷ panel, this page) has 200 slot machines, three blackjack tables, one poker table and two roulette wheels. Guests must be over 18.
🏠 G8 ✉ Avenida do Infante ☎ 291 209 180 🕔 Sun–Thu 3–3, Fri–Sat 4–4

CITYSIGHTSEEING FUNCHAL
www.city-sightseeing.com
Tickets for these hop-on-hop-off open-top sightseeing buses are valid for 24 hours. This company's route takes in more sights than that of its competitor.
☎ 919 558 856 🕔 Daily 9.30–5.30

ENGLISH CHURCH
www.holytrinity-madeira.org
This neoclassical church hosts regular, widely advertised classical concerts and other cultural events. Tickets can be obtained from Funchal's tourist office.
🏠 a1 ✉ Rua Quebra Costas 18 ☎ 291 220 674

FRENTE MAR FUNCHAL
This is a purpose-built area encompassing the Lido, promenade, Ponta Gorda resort and the parks and gardens that line the coast to the west of the city centre. Facilities and public areas are maintained to very high standards and there are many bars and restaurants.
🏠 G8 ✉ Ponta Gorda ☎ 291 706 950 🕔 Opening

times vary from site to site
🖥 1, 2, 4, 6, 12

GAVIÃO YACHT
Offering a more upmarket and personalized experience than many of the marina-based boat trip companies, this yacht takes up to 20 people on half-day wildlife-spotting trips, mini-cruises to the Desertas and on romantic sunset excursions around the bay.
🏠 b3 ✉ Marina do Funchal ☎ 291 241 124

M. GAVINA FISHING TRIPS
Skipper Miguel Gavina specializes in big game fishing trips aboard the Hawk Eye. Blue marlin and tuna are the most common types of fish caught.
🏠 b3 ✉ Marina do Funchal ☎ 291 238 422

MADEIRA CATAMARAN
www.madeiracatamaran.com
Hop on board one of this company's two catamarans (Sea Pleasure and Sea the Best) for an enjoyable cruise combining wildlife-watching, swimming, snorkelling, sunbathing and simply island gazing. The company offers a free second trip if you don't spot any wildlife on your first excursion.
🏠 b3 ✉ Marina do Funchal ☎ 291 224 900 🕔 Daily 10.30–3, 3–6.30pm (weather permitting)

MINI ECO BAR

This is a trendy retro bar serving teas, coffees and snacks such as toasted sandwiches, as well as *poncha* (cocktail made from sugar-cane spirit, honey and lemon juice) to laid-back vibes and live DJs at weekends. There's free WiFi and a friendly welcome.

✚ b2 ✉ Rua de Alfândega 3 ☎ 934 838 866 🕐 Mon–Tue 9pm–midnight, Wed–Fri 9am–3am, Sat 10am–2pm, 9pm–3am

O'BRIENS

This large Irish pub attracts a faithful ex-pat and tourist clientele who come to enjoy sport on big-screen TVs while downing pints of Guinness. There's live music on some nights and a golfers' corner.

✚ G8 ✉ Estrada Monumental, 175–177 ☎ 291 717 600 🕐 noon–late 🚌 1, 2, 4, 6, 12

PESTANA TOUR KIOSK

Located near the casino, this tour agency runs a range of excellent island tours, including hikes to Pico Ruivo and various *levada* walks led by qualified mountain guides. It prefers to keep groups small and its prices are reasonable. It will also arrange pick-ups from your hotel.

✚ G8 ✉ Avenida do Infante ☎ 291 232 028 🕐 Daily 9.30–7

PORTO SANTO GOLF COURSE

If you are visiting Porto Santo (▷ 37) and enjoy golf, this18-hole course (par 72) comprises two distinctly different areas—an American-style South Course, which is landscaped with lakes and trees, and the cliff-top North Course. There is also a 9-hole pitch and putt course that is ideal for beginners.

✚ BII ✉ Porto Santo ☎ 291 983 778 🕐 Daily 9.30–5.30

PRINCE ALBERT PUB

This is a wonderful Victorian-style pub run by an amiable Welshman. It is the most authentic British pub in town, serving good pub grub while you watch the latest on Sky Sports. Also offers occasional live music.

✚ G8 ✉ Rua Imperatriz

TAKE A TOUR

Countless travel agents and hotels offer tours of the island. Most visitors plump for an east or west tour, the Curral das Freiras, otherwise known as the Nuns' Valley (▷ 54) or a *levada* walk. Avoid tours that take in east and west in one day as you'll spend most of your time on the coach. Also, be very wary of free tours as you may find yourself inspecting a time-share complex at the end of the day.

D. Amélia ☎ 291 235 793 🕐 9am–late, Sun 11am–late

PUB NO. 2

An inconspicuous tavern that is frequented by locals and foreigners alike. It serves British and Portuguese beers and basic dishes in simple surroundings.

✚ G8 ✉ Rua da Favilla 2 ☎ 291 230 676 🕐 Daily 10am–2am

SANTA MARIA DE COLOMBO

www.madeirapirateboat.com This pint-sized replica of *Santa Maria*, the ship on which Christopher Columbus sailed to the Americas, takes you along the coast from Funchal for a mixture of wildlife-spotting, swimming and sightseeing. There is an on-board bar plus free wine and *bolo de mel*.

✚ b3 ✉ Marina do Funchal ☎ 291 220 327 🕐 Daily 10.30–1..30, 3–6

VESPAS NIGHTCLUB

www.discotecavespas.com This is Funchal's only bona fide nightclub and it is Madeira's liveliest nightspot by far. Saturday is the best night to get on down in the company of the big-name DJs who appear here. Things start very late here and don't wrap up until around breakfast time.

✚ a3 ✉ Avenida Sá Carneiro 7 ☎ 291 234 800 🕐 Wed 11pm–5.30am, Fri–Sat 11pm–7am

Restaurants

ADEGA A CUBA (€)

This is a great lunch spot with an inexpensive set menu. The ambience is rustic, with chairs and bar stools, as well as a section of the dining area, cut from old barrels.
➕ b2 ✉ Rua do Bispo 28 ☎ 291 220 986 🕐 Daily 8am–10pm

APOLO (€€)

www.apolorestaurante.com
Situated just outside the Cathedral, this Funchal institution has an art deco interior and an attractive terrace. Serves a wide choice of international dishes and Madeiran specialities.
➕ b2 ✉ Rua Dr. J. António Almeida 21 ☎ 291 220 099 🕐 Daily 8am–11pm

ARMAZÉM DO SAL (€€€)

www.armazemdosal.com
Occupying a 400-year-old salt store, this is one of Funchal's best restaurants. The menu is Madeiran-Argentine fusion, and the service and wine list are outstanding.
➕ c2 ✉ Rua da Alfândega · 135 ☎ 291 241 285 🕐 Mon–Fri 12–12, Sat dinner only

ARSENIOS (€€–€€€)

Come to this famous and atmospheric dining hall between 8 and 10pm to hear live *fado* while you tuck into succulent meat grilled to perfection.
➕ e2 ✉ Rua de Santa Maria 169 ☎ 291 224 007 🕐 Daily noon–2am

BEATLES BOAT (€€)

Housed in and around a boat once owned by the Fab Four (though they never visited Madeira), and now set in concrete, this is a bit of a tourist trap but an interesting experience all the same.
➕ c3 ✉ Avenida do Mar ☎ 291 223 572 🕐 Daily lunch, dinner

BEERHOUSE (€€€)

Located on a pier at the marina, this brew pub ferments its own cloudy wheat beer. Great beer, pricey food.

FIND YOUR FISH

Some menus have only the Portuguese names for fish or give incorrect translations. Here are some you might encounter: *atum* (tuna); *bacalhau* (salted cod); *cherne* (sea bass); *carapau* (mackerel); *pargo* (bream); *salmão* (salmon); *salmonete* (red mullet); *truta* (trout); *espadarte* (swordfish); and *espada* (scabbard fish)–the long and scary black sea creature from the deepest depths of the Atlantic.

➕ b3 ✉ Marina do Funchal ☎ 291 229 011 🕐 Daily 10am–late

A BICA (€€)

Packing diners in like sardines at the fish market opposite, this no-nonsense restaurant caters to market traders and occasional tourists. It serves generous portions of scabbard and steak and inexpensive set lunches.
➕ d2 ✉ Rua Hospital Velho 17 ☎ 291 221 346 🕐 Mon–Sat lunch, dinner

CAFÉ DO MUSEU (€)

Attractively set within the eight basalt arches of the Sacred Art Museum (▷ 28), this museum café dishes up tasty sandwiches, fish, steaks and salads as well as inexpensive set lunches. Minimalist dining room, plus an outdoor terrace.
➕ b2 ✉ Praça do Municipio ☎ 291 281 121 🕐 Daily 9.30am–2am

CAFÉ DO TEATRO (€€)

www.cafedoteatro.com
This trendy garden-café at the Baltazar Dias Theatre serves snacks and drinks by day and cocktails to DJ sessions by night.
➕ b2 ✉ Avenida Arriaga ☎ 291 226 371 🕐 Mon–Fri 8am–1am, Sat–Sun 10am–late

CASA ITÁLIA (€€)

Good pizzas, pasta, *gelato* and salads are served in what most agree is Madeira's

most authentic Italian ambience.

➕ G8 ✉ Rua de Gorgulho 16 ☎ 291 776 510
🕐 Daily 11am–midnight

CASA MADEIRENSE (€€€)

www.casamadeirense-funchal. com

Done out in terracotta, red leather and *azulejos*, this lively eatery is a good place to come for local cuisine, especially if you are staying in Funchal's hotel zone.

➕ G8 ✉ Estrada Monumental 153 ☎ 291 766 700 🕐 Daily 11am–2am
🚌 1, 2, 4, 6, 12

CASA VELHA (€€€)

The multi-tasking 'Old House' is atmospheric and welcoming, with an intimate restaurant upstairs and a relaxing bar and overgrown garden downstairs. The menu features international classics as well as a choice of Madeiran staples.

➕ G8 ✉ Rua Imperatriz D. Amélia 69 ☎ 291 205 604
🕐 Daily lunch, dinner

CIDADE VELHA (€€)

Classic Madeiran dishes such as salted cod with cornmeal crust, and a wonderful outdoor seating area next to the sea and fort, make this a particularly attractive dining option. Reservations are advised.

➕ e3 ✉ Rua Portão de Santiago ☎ 291 232 021
🕐 Daily 10am–midnight

DONA AMÉLIA (€€€)

Elegant and understated, this fine-dining establishment near the casino offers top-notch Madeiran cooking at neatly laid tables with sea views. The service here is as good as it gets on the island.

➕ G8 ✉ Rua Imperatriz D. Amélia 83 ☎ 291 225 784
🕐 Daily lunch, dinner

É PRÁ PICANHA (€€)

www.eprapicanha.com

This contemporary place on the hotel zone's main drag specializes in churrasco steak (marinated in a peppery sauce and barbecued), though fish, lamb and kid are also on the menu. Good wine list.

➕ G8 ✉ Avenida do Infante 60A ☎ 291 282 257 🕐 Daily lunch, dinner 🚌 1, 2, 4, 6, 12

FIM DO SÉCULO (€–€€)

Munch on Madeira staples in the stone and *azulejos*-lined interior, or

SNACKS TO GO

Madeira is a place to explore on foot and all that walking can leave you feeling peckish. When it's time to grab a snack, options include *bolo de caco*, a chewy wheat bread served hot with assorted fillings; roasted sweet chestnuts from the forests around Curral das Freiras; and *pasteis de nata* (custard tarts) available from any bakery for a few cents.

grab a seat on pedestrianized Carreira for a spot of people-watching while you eat. The lunch menu offers superb value.

➕ b2 ✉ Rua da Carreira 144 ☎ 291 224 476 🕐 Mon–Sat lunch, dinner

IL GALLO D'ORO (€€€)

Proudly sporting a Michelin star, the restaurant at the Cliff Bay Hotel may not impress with its ordinary decor, but the Mediterranean food is first-rate. Men are expected to wear a jacket and tie.

➕ G8 ✉ Estrada Monumental 147 ☎ 291 707 700 🕐 Daily breakfast, dinner
🚌 1, 2, 4, 6, 12

GAVIÃO NOVO (€€€)

Wedged into a narrow house in the Zona Velha, this tiny, very popular restaurant specializes in succulent grilled lamb, seafood and steaks. Reservations are highly recommended.

➕ e2 ✉ Rua de Santa Maria 131 ☎ 291 229 238 🕐 Daily 12–11

GRAND CAFÉ GOLDEN GATE (€€€)

This colonial-style café-bar, with lots of wicker and dark wood, is an atmospheric spot for a light lunch, cocktails or your first and last coffee of the day.

➕ b2 ✉ Avenida Arriaga 29 ☎ 291 234 383 🕐 Mon–Sat 8am–11pm, Sun 10am–11pm

O JANGO (€€)

www.ojango.net

O Jango is an Angolan word meaning a thatched hut, and this place has a mildly African theme. This 100-seater restaurant—big for the Zona Velha—serves a good range of meat, shellfish and fish.

✚ e2 ✉ Rua de Santa Maria 162 ☎ 291 221 280 🕔 Daily 11–11

LAREIRA PORTUGUESA (€€€)

A refreshingly contemporary place just off Estrada Monumental, where you can enjoy black scabbard caviar, octopus, lobster and meat dishes.

✚ G8 ✉ Travessa Dr. Valente 7 (Estrada Monumental) ☎ 291 762 911 🕔 Daily lunch, dinner 🚍 1, 2, 4, 6, 12

LEQUE (€)

This is a local favourite for light snacks, coffees and juices. It is always busy, and the waitresses don't stop from dawn till dusk. Escape the busy interior for a spot on the *praça*.

✚ b2 ✉ Praça do Município 7 ☎ 291 224 229 🕔 Daily 8am–10pm

MOMENTOS GOURMET (€€)

Situated in the heart of the hotel zone, this snazzy newcomer is a world away from Madeira's traditional eateries. Minimalist design lends an up-to-the-minute ambience and the menu is a mix of Portuguese classics, such as cod with cornmeal crust, and international dishes with an Italian twist. There's a terrace for warm evenings.

✚ H8 ✉ Rua Ponta da Cruz 12A ☎ 291 098 252 🕔 Daily 10.30am–2am

A MURALHA (€€)

Encased in glass, this popular spot specializes in *espetada* on laurel spits and succulent tuna steaks. There are also vegetarian options and a children's menu, as well as good value set lunches and daily specials.

✚ e2 ✉ Largo do Corpo Santo ☎ 291 232 561 🕔 Daily lunch, dinner

OLIVES (€€)

Take a seat at one of the tightly packed tables for well-prepared mains and mouth-watering desserts, all rinsed down with a glass or two of Portuguese wine. Service can be slow.

✚ c2 ✉ Rua da Queimada de Cima 47 ☎ 291 236 004 🕔 Mon–Sat 10am–midnight

PENHA D'AGUIA (€)

This is the best bakery in the city centre. Good for a quick coffee or a pastry blow-out. Ask them to box up a selection of pastries to take away.

✚ c2 ✉ Rua de João Gago 6–8 ☎ 291 228 119 🕔 Mon–Fri 8–7, Sat–Sun 8–1.30

O PORTÃO (€€)

Buried deep in the Zona Velha, this tightly packed eatery specializes in flambéed steak, cooked at your table. Dishes are very reasonably priced and many customers make repeat visits.

✚ e3 ✉ Rua Portão De Sao Tiago ☎ 291 221 125 🕔 Daily 11–11

QASBAH (€€)

A Thai Buddha in the doorway and Moroccan tiles lining the dining area send mixed messages, but the food is definitely North African with lots of couscous, tagines and kebabs. The terrace has amazing Atlantic views. Situated west of the Lido.

✚ G8 ✉ Promenade do Lido ☎ 291 765 500 🕔 Daily 11am–midnight 🚍 1, 2, 4, 6, 12

BOLO DE MEL

Madeirans' favourite tooth-rotter is *bolo de mel*, often called 'honey cake' though it is actually made using *mel de cana* (molasses). Other ingredients include flour, nuts, almonds, dried fruit and spices, and the result is something between British Christmas pudding and a rich ginger cake. It should not be confused with Madeira cake, which acquired its misleading name in Britain, where it was a popular accompaniment to Madeira wine.

QUINTA PALMEIRA (€€€)

Occupying an elegant 18th-century *quinta*, the Palmeira specializes in Madeiran fine dining in romantic surroundings.
🔂 G8 ✉ Avenida do Infante 17/19 ☎ 291 221 814 🕓 Daily lunch, dinner 🚌 1, 2, 4, 6, 12

O REGIONAL (€€€)

This modern seafood restaurant is the best of a bunch near the Madeira Story Centre. Scabbard with banana and pork medallions with sweet potato are recommended.
🔂 d2 ✉ Rua D. Carlos I 54 ☎ 291 232 956 🕓 Daily 11.30–11

REID'S TEA TERRACE (€€€)

www.reidspalace.com
At €28 a shot, afternoon tea (finger sandwiches, scones, cakes and speciality teas) at Reid's Hotel is expensive, but the location on the terrace and the views across Funchal make it (almost) worth it. Reservations are a must and smart-casual attire is recommended.
🔂 G8 ✉ Reid's Hotel, Estrada Monumental 139 ☎ 291 717 171 🕓 Daily 3–5.30 🚌 1, 2, 4, 6, 12

RISO (€€)

Riso means rice in Portuguese, and many variations on this theme are what you'll find on the menu here. It has a superb location, clinging

to the side of the São Tiago Fort with stunning sea views.
🔂 e3 ✉ Rua de Santa Maria 274 ☎ 291 280 360 🕓 Mon–Sat 10–5.30, 7–12

SÃO PEDRO (€€)

Located opposite the beautiful Church of São Pedro, this contemporary, family-run eatery is good at any time of the day—for a quick coffee break between sights or for an evening meal with drinks. Madeiran specialities dominate the menu.
🔂 b1 ✉ Rua São Pedro 2–4 ☎ 291 222 217 🕓 Daily 6am–11pm

TAJ MAHAL (€€)

Enjoy the full range of Madras, *vindaloo*, korma and balti dishes at Madeira's top Indian restaurant. Atlantic vistas as well.
🔂 G8 ✉ Rua Imperatriz D. Amélia 119 ☎ 291 228 038 🕓 Daily lunch, dinner

MINIBUS INCLUDED

Many off-the-beaten-track restaurants offer customers a minibus service from their hotel. Restaurateurs do this in order to stop taxi drivers from taking punters to restaurants where they get commission. They also understand that negotiating Madeira's steep and twisting roads at night, or working out how to get a bus to the restaurant, can be off-putting.

O TAPASSOL (€€)

www.restaurantetapassol.com
This is a real Zona Velha treat with snugly arranged tables, a sunny terrace, hardwood floors, whitewashed walls and flower-filled window boxes. Options include wild boar, rabbit and catch of the day. Reservations advised.
🔂 e2 ✉ Rua D. Carlos I 62 ☎ 291 225 023 🕓 Daily 11–11

TOKOS (€€€)

www.restaurantetokos.com
Occupying a traditional house with a rambling garden in the hotel zone, Tokos is primarily known for its seafood, including imaginative versions of old classics, and flambée dishes. Also serves steaks, veal and pork.
🔂 G8 ✉ Estrada Monumental 169 ☎ 291 771 019 🕓 Tue–Sat lunch, dinner, Sun dinner only 🚌 1, 2, 4, 6, 12

VILLA CIPRIANI (€€€)

www.reidspalace.com
Choose from a short menu of finely crafted Italian dishes as you enjoy the brief but spectacular sunset from the cliff-top terrace of the Italian restaurant in Reid's Palace hotel. Smart casual attire is required and reservations are recommended.
🔂 G8 ✉ Estrada Monumental 139 ☎ 291 717 171 🕓 Daily dinner only 🚌 1, 2, 4, 6, 12

From the heights of Monte to the beach at Câmara de Lobos and the lush Botanical Gardens, nothing in southern Madeira is more than a short bus ride from downtown Funchal. Inland, Curral das Freiras offers a taste of the mountainous interior.

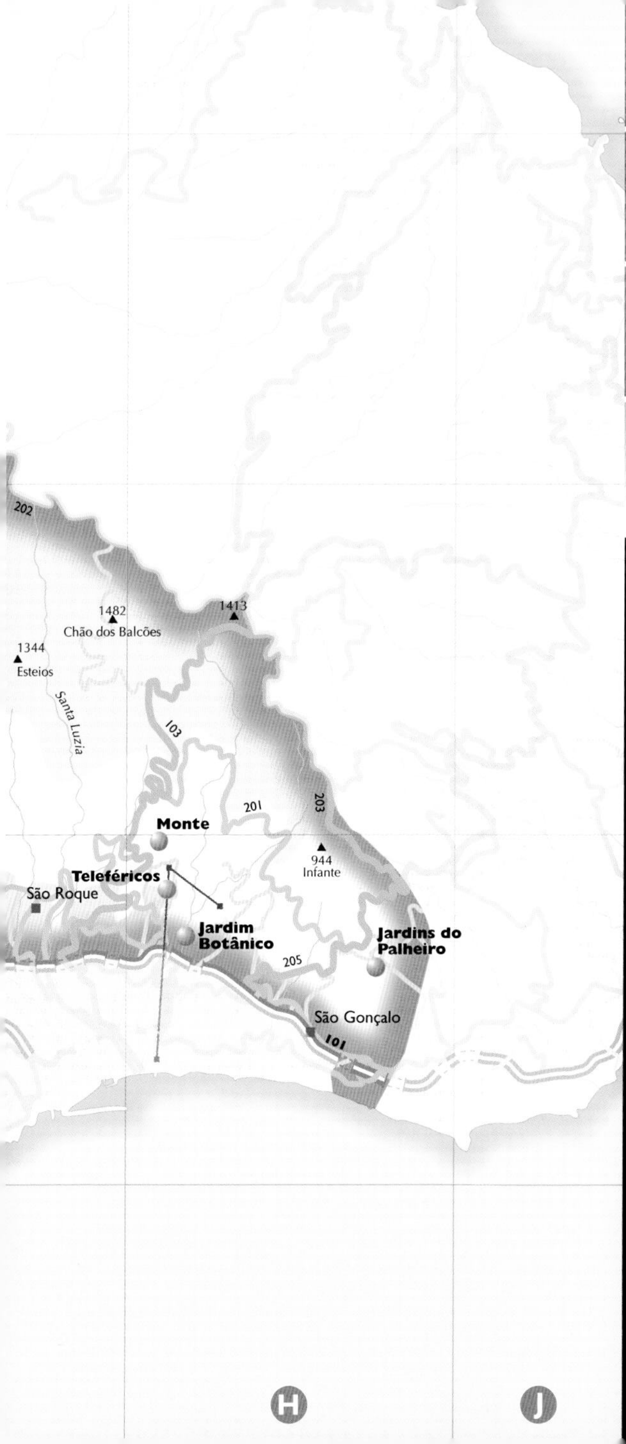

202

1482
▲
Chão dos Balcões

1413
▲

1344
▲
Esteios

Santa Luzia

103

201

203

Monte

944
▲
Infante

Teleféricos

São Roque

Jardim Botânico

205

Jardins do Palheiro

São Gonçalo

101

H

J

Cabo Girão

TOP 25

High views over the sea and fertile terraces at Cabo Girão, a dramatic promontory

THE BASICS

- F8
- 15km (9 miles) west of Funchal
- Café
- 154
- Few

HIGHLIGHTS

- Heart-stopping cliff-top views from the *miradouro*
- Photographic exhibition on early tourism in Madeira

TIP

- The bus timetable makes a half-day trip impossible at weekends, so plan for a weekday if you are dependent on public transport.

Soaring high above a sapphire Atlantic, with dizzying views east to Funchal and beyond, these sea cliffs are some of the tallest in the world.

U-turn This colossal hunk of volcanic rock was the point at which the Portuguese explorer Zarco turned back on his first sortie along the coast of Madeira in 1418; in fact, Cabo Girão means 'Cape of Return'. Entries in Zarco's diary indicate that he was pretty bowled over by these cliffs, which soar more than half a kilo-metre (580m/1,900ft) into the sky. Depending on your definition of a sea cliff, this makes Cabo Girão the second (or seventh) highest in Europe; local guides tend to prefer the former.

Peering into the abyss However you arrive at Cabo Girão, a short walk through the small car park and a fragrant stretch of eucalyptus wood brings you to the *miradouro* or lookout point. The railings are set unnervingly close to the edge, allowing visitors to point their camera straight down into the abyss. Snapshots of a thin white line of waves breaking against the shore below look as though they were taken from a plane window. The minuscule terraces and fields are now reached by boat, but in the past farmers lowered themselves down on ropes to tend these fertile, south-facing plots. Back at the car park a basic café shares premises with a free exhibition of black and white photographs depicting tourism on Madeira in years gone by.

Boats pulled up on the beach at Câmara de Lobos, a picturesque fishing village (right)

Câmara de Lobos

This traditional fishing village is rowdy with hard-working fishermen, who bring in the night's catch then kick back with a nip of something strong. Winston Churchill once captured the picturesque scene on canvas.

Fish tales Pretty Câmara de Lobos is the centre of the scabbard fishing industry. By day, fishing boats hauled up on the beach add a dash of colour, but come nightfall the fleet embarks on its all-night search for the scabbard, using lines almost a kilometre long. With the catch safely packed off to Funchal, the fishermen resume their boozing in the bars, where the favourite local tipple is *poncha*, a concoction of cane spirit, honey and lemon juice.

Churchill's retreat What does an ex-prime minister do when he's won a war but lost an election? Set up easel above the harbour in a Madeiran fishing village, of course. In 1950, while pondering his future and emptying bottles of Madeira, Churchill depicted Câmara de Lobos in oil, producing paintings which now fetch six-figure sums at auction. He returned to Britain for the 1951 general election and won a second term in office.

Pray-as-you-go One stop in the village is the baroque Capela Nossa Senhora da Conçeição (Chapel of Our Lady), where fishermen pray for safe deliverance and a plentiful catch before setting out onto the fickle *Atlântico*.

THE BASICS

➕ F8

✉ 9km (5 miles) west of Funchal

🍴 Numerous restaurants, cafés, bars

🚌 6, 7, 27, 80, 137, 146,154

♿ Few

ℹ Rua Padre Clemente Nunes Pereira, tel 291 943 470

HIGHLIGHTS

● Scenes admired and painted by Winston Churchill
● Wandering through the quaint narrow lanes around the harbour

TIP

● From the eastern end of Câmara de Lobos there are spectacular views of Cabo Girão (▷ 52), just a few kilometres along the coast.

Curral das Freiras

HIGHLIGHTS

● Views of the mountain-scape and village from Eira do Serrado
● Local chestnut specialities served in the village cafés and bars

TIP

● The old road to Curral das Freiras from Eira do Serrado is now closed, although it is still shown on some maps. To continue, trace your route back to the main road and take the tunnel.

Huddling in a cauldron of mountains, Curral das Freiras offers dramatic views and an eventful history, making it a popular day-trip destination from Funchal.

Sister act Curral das Freiras translates as 'nuns' refuge', as it was to this inaccessible spot, encircled by vertical peaks, that Funchal's nuns took flight in 1566 when the island was attacked by pirates. Though the sisters returned to their convent in Funchal when the danger passed, the village they founded in the mountains continued to grow. Incredibly, until 1959, when a road was built, its only link to the outside world was a zigzagging path down the hillside. This trail is still an interesting way to reach the village—though don't expect to have it to yourself.

A retreat of 16th-century nuns fleeing pirates, Curral das Freiras is a hidden gem deep in the mountains northwest of Funchal

Highs and lows Whether driving yourself or taking a tour, the first stop en route to Curral das Freiras should be Pico dos Barcelos (355m/1,165ft), a *miradouro* providing sweeping Funchal vistas. From there, road ER107 twists through the forest to the turn-off for Eira do Serrado (before the new tunnel). This lookout point perches 800m (2,600ft) above Curral das Freiras, offering widescreen views of the natural amphitheatre and the village at the bottom. From here, hike the path down to the village (allow 90 minutes: you could take a taxi back if you don't want to walk both ways) or drive back to the ER107, which tunnels through the mountains to the village. Either way, relax in one of the village cafés with a *licor de castanha* (chestnut liqueur), made with sweet chestnuts from the surrounding forest.

THE BASICS

✚ F7
✉ 12km (7 miles) north-west of Funchal
🍴 Restaurants and cafés
🚌 81
♿ Few
❓ The village celebrates Festa da Castanha (Chestnut Festival) in November

Jardim Botânico

TOP
25

Swathed year-round in a rich carpet of subtropical greenery, Madeira is often dubbed 'the island of eternal spring'. Nowhere is this more striking than in the intriguing botanical gardens.

Green shoots The Quinta de Bom Sucesso was built by the Reid family (founders of Reid's Palace Hotel) as their private residence. In the 1950s the mansion and surrounding gardens were acquired by the regional government, which transformed them into the Botanical Gardens you see today. The *quinta* became the now rather tired Natural History Museum, while the already magnificent hillside gardens were sown with a multitude of indigenous and tropical plants, shrubs, trees and flowers. The gardens were opened to the public in 1960

Clockwise from left: overview of the Jardim Botânico, a gorgeous arrangement of colour, pattern and texture; close-up of the geometrically designed herb garden; corner of the cacti garden; visitors admiring the precision planting

and have since become one of Madeira's must-see attractions.

Floral delights Pathways, steps and archways funnel visitors from one level of terracing to the next as they ogle the vast array of plant life on display. Star of the show in the cooler months (late November to early April) are the orchids. Other highlights are the cacti garden with its sculptural succulents and three dimensional spider's webs, the indigenous plants section showcasing species from across the Madeiran archipelago, and the topiary garden. A *mira-douro* on the western side of the gardens overlooks the Ribeira de João Gomes gorge, but the view is spoilt by a bridge feeding traffic into a tunnel under the Botanical Gardens—controversial additions to the cityscape.

THE BASICS

www.madeirabotanical garden.com
🞧 H8
✉ Caminho do Meio
☎ 291 211 200
🕔 Daily 9–5.30
🍴 Café
🚌 29, 30, 31
♿ None
💲 Inexpensive

Monte

TOP 25

Monte Palace and the Jardim do Monte, one of the finest gardens on Madeira

THE BASICS

🔲 H8

✉ 6km (4 miles) north of Funchal

🍽 Restaurants and cafés on Largo da Fonte and Caminho do Monte

🚌 20, 21, 48

♿ Few

❓ Feast of the Assumption, 15 Aug

Monte Palace Gardens

🔲 H8

✉ Caminho do Monte 174

🕐 Daily 9.30–6

🚌 20, 21, 48, cable car from Jardim Botânico and central Funchal

♿ Few

✋ Expensive

HIGHLIGHT

● The double-spired, white-washed and basalt church of Our Lady of Monte

---

TIP

● If you are here on the Feast of the Assumption (15 August) visit in the evening when there are fireworks and free concerts.

Olde-worlde yet chic, the hillside town of Monte oozes charm. It has changed little since its Victorian heyday.

Old-style charisma With a cable car ascent for starter (▷ 61), and a toboggan ride (▷ 59) for after, the main course is this fascinating little town with its vistas, villas and pebbled squares. Once a health spa for the well-to-do, this was the main hub of tourism prior to World War II, but when the funicular railway was discontinued Funchal began to steal the show, leaving Monte elegantly preserved. This is best illustrated on pretty Largo da Fonte, where the former railway station looks across to the old fountain pavilion. Over the centuries many *quintas* were built in and around Monte, including the Monte Palace to the south of the square. In 1987 the grounds were transformed into the Jardim do Monte (Monte Palace Gardens), some of the finest gardens on the island.

Last emperor Top billing in Monte goes to the Church of Our Lady of Monte (Igreja de Nossa Senhora do Monte). Inside, the statue of the Virgin, purportedly discovered by a shepherdess in nearby Terreira da Luta in the 15th century, is the focus of the Feast of the Assumption (15 August). A chapel to the left as you enter the church holds the tomb of the last Austrian Emperor, Charles I. Living in exile in Madeira after World War I, he died of tuberculosis in Monte, his casket a far-flung full stop to the Habsburg story.

The Monte toboggan ride is guaranteed to get the pulse racing

TOP 25

Monte: Toboggan Ride

If hurtling down steep lanes in a wicker basket, steered loosely in the right direction by men in straw hats, sounds like fun, then this classic Madeira experience may be for you.

White-knuckle ride The two-seater toboggans mounted on oiled wooden runners slip and slide down the steep route from the Church of Our Lady of Monte to the Funchal suburb of Livramento (approximately 2km/1 mile), with two 'drivers' keeping things on course on the sharp bends. The drivers wear goatskin boots with pieces of old car tyre gummed to the bottom to help them gain leverage against the toboggan. Some people will have no better fun on Madeira, but others regard it as an over-priced gimmick designed to part holidaymakers with their euros. Most cruise ships calling at Funchal offer this brief experience as a shore excursion, but much of the time the toboggans are stacked up unused, the few would-be punters put off by the high fare.

Push and shove The toboggans are the last remnant of a means of transport common across Madeira until road construction began. Goods and occasionally people were transported from place to place on runners, a much more practical solution than wheels in Madeira's steep and rocky landscape. Around the island, see if you can spot rounded flights of steps lined with pebbles, designed to make it easier for toboggans to negotiate awkward terrain.

THE BASICS

🚩 H8
✉ Caminho do Monte, Monte
🕐 Mon–Sat 9–6, Sun 9–1
🍴 Restaurants and cafés on Largo da Fonte and Caminho do Monte
🚌 20, 21, 48
♿ None
💰 Expensive

HIGHLIGHT

● The heart-pumping thrill of the ride

TIPS

● Many visitors travel up to Monte by cable car and down again by toboggan and bus.
● The price doesn't include the drivers' tip.
● You'd be very fortunate to bargain down the fare, but have a go anyway.

 TOP 25

Jardins do Palheiro

Planted in the English style, the Jardins do Palheiro have 'garden rooms' and topiary

THE BASICS

www.palheiroestate.com

H8

São Gonçalo, exit 13 on motorway, 8km (5 miles) east of Funchal

291 793 044

Mon–Fri 9–4.30

Tea house

36, 37

Few

Expensive

HIGHLIGHTS

● The camellia gardens when they are in flower (Nov–Apr)
● Enjoying afternoon tea in the Tea House

TIP

● The estate also encompasses a superb 18-hole, par 72 golf course and hotel with spa.

Commonly known as Blandy's, these English formal gardens a few kilometres east of Funchal are some of the finest gardens on the island.

Aristocratic origins The Palheiro Ferreiro estate was established by the Portuguese Count of Carvalhal in the early part of the 19th century. Having built a *quinta* and a baroque chapel, he surrounded them with gardens planted mostly with trees. The count fled to England during the Portuguese Civil War of the early1830s, and there encountered the English garden. On his return, he refashioned his own estate in the English style. In 1884 the estate was acquired by the rich and powerful Blandy family of wine merchants; they made it their main residence and introduced plants from all over the world.

Blooming marvellous Wandering the pathways, you will encounter an international roster of plants—Japanese flowering shrubs, trees from China, Redwoods from California, Candelabra trees from Brazil, proteas from South Africa and most of Madeira's own flora. Camellias, introduced to Madeira in about 1810, are a particular feature of the estate. The gardens are pruned into 'rooms' divided by hedges in the English style, with the exception of one wooded ravine, known as Hell *(Inferno)*, which has been left to grow naturally. A path winding through this cool part of the gardens passes huge tree ferns from New Zealand.

Take an exhilarating ride on the Teleféricos, running high over valleys east of Funchal

Teleféricos

Dangling high above the city's red rooftops, Madeira's cable cars are both a tourist attraction and a vital mode of transport on the island.

Don't look down The state-of-the-art, Austrian-built cable car system first took to the skies above Funchal in 2000. The main cable car (Teleféricos da Madeira) ascends 550m (1,800ft) from the eastern end of the seafront to Monte, a journey of 15 minutes. The success of this route meant it was soon joined by a second (Teleféricos do Jardim Botânico), which soars from Monte to the Botanical Gardens (▷ 56), spanning the valley of the River João Gomes along the way and taking nine minutes to complete the journey. The *teleféricos* cuts out long-winded trips through the steep and snaking streets of Funchal's eastern suburbs, and has reduced traffic throughout the city.

Forerunner The *teleféricos* was a long awaited replacement (60 years!) for the rack and pinion funicular that trundled from Funchal to Terreiro da Luta via Monte. Discontinued in 1939 after several engine explosions, it was never reinstated. The tracks were quickly ripped up, but some remnants of the railway survive, such as the viaduct, and the derelict station building and ticket kiosk on Monte's Largo da Fonte (▷ 58). There has been talk of rebuilding the railway for many years, but so far this has come to nothing. Rua do Comboio follows the route of the old line.

THE BASICS

Teleféricos da Madeira
* H8
* Avenida do Mar, Funchal
* 291 780 280
* Daily 10–6
* Cafés
* Good
* Expensive

Teleféricos do Jardim Botânico
* H8
* Largo das Barbosas, Monte; Caminha das Voltas, Funchal
* 291 210 290
* Daily 9.30–6
* Café at Botanical Gardens
* Good
* Moderate

HIGHLIGHT

● Soaring high above the ravines east of Funchal

TIP

● Take the Teleféricos up to Monte and then Bus 20, or a combination of toboggan and bus, back to Funchal.

Restaurants

PRICES

Prices are approximate, based on a 3-course meal for one person.

€€€   over €25
€€   €15–€25
€   under €15

ALTO MONTE (€)

A popular spot for tourists waiting to take the bus back into Funchal, the 'High Monte' does a good line in light snacks, sandwiches and drinks, and has great views from its terrace.

➕ H8 ✉ Travessa das Tilias, Monte ☎ 291 782 261 ⏰ Daily 8–8 🚌 20, 21, 48

CAFÉ DE PARQUE (€)

The perfect place to linger over a long cool drink and write postcards home, this delightfully olde-worlde café is well situated on Monte's attractive main square.

➕ H8 ✉ Largo da Fonte, Monte ☎ 291 782 880 ⏰ Daily 9–6 🚌 20, 21, 48

CAFÉ REPÚBLICA (€)

Part of the modern development at the western end of Câmara de Lobos, this simple café is a decent spot for light snacks if you find the fishermen-filled bars near the harbour become a bit overwhelming.

➕ F8 ✉ Praça da Autonomia, Câmara de Lobos ☎ 291 941 083 ⏰ Daily 7am–2am 🚌 6, 7, 27, 80, 137, 146, 154

CANTINHO DOS MARISCOS (€€€)

Minimalist decor, views of Cabo Girão and some unusual modern twists on local seafood dishes make this a smart choice in Câmara de Lobos.

➕ F8 ✉ Praça da Autonomia, Câmara de Lobos ☎ 291 943 125 ⏰ Daily 12–11 🚌 6, 7, 27, 80, 137, 146, 154

CHURCHILL (€€€)

This fish restaurant is the obvious choice in Câmara de Lobos, and customers are greeted at the door. Choose from the sunny terrace with harbour views or the attractive dining room.

➕ F8 ✉ Estrada João Gonçalves Zarco 39, Câmara de Lobos ☎ 291 941 451 ⏰ Daily 10–10 🚌 6, 7, 27, 80, 137, 146, 154

HENRIQUE & HENRIQUE

When in Câmara de Lobos, why not visit this reputable wine lodge belonging to one of the largest producers on Madeira? The wines on sale, including the classic four Madeiras (Bual, Verdelho, Sercial and Malmsey) are regarded as some of the best around, and many can be tasted for free. To find Henrique & Henrique (Mon–Fri 9–1, 2.30–5.30), head up Rua de Santa until you see the barrels behind large glass windows.

QUINTA DO MONTE (€€€)

Monte's finest eatery, the restaurant at the five-star Hotel Quinta do Monte maintains an air of aristocratic tranquillity. The à la carte dishes are served in a modern but understated conservatory or outside in the tropical gardens.

➕ H8 ✉ Caminho do Monte 192/194 ☎ 291 724 236 ⏰ Daily lunch, dinner 🚌 20, 21, 48

VALE DAS FREIRAS (€)

This restaurant doesn't look much from the outside, but the stone-clad interior is comfortable and the terrace offers incredible views down through the valley. From the limited menu, Nuns' Chestnuts, sourced from the local mountains, are a must for a starter, and chestnut liqueur makes a great *digestif*.

➕ F7 ✉ Curral das Freiras ☎ 969 902 690 ⏰ Daily 9–7 🚌 81

VILA DO PEIXE (€€€)

The ultra-modern glass facade affords spectacular views to accompany the well-prepared fish and seafood. Meat dishes are also available and there are some vegetarian options too.

➕ F8 ✉ Rua Dr. João Abel de Freitas 30, Câmara de Lobos ☎ 291 099 909 ⏰ Daily 10–midnight 🚌 6, 7, 27, 80, 137, 146, 154

If bagging peaks, hitting trails and general outdoor fun appeals to you, make a beeline for Central Madeira, a dramatic landscape of sharp-toothed volcanic rock, sheer valleys and dense forest. The north coast is also rugged, with villages clinging to wind-lashed cliff tops.

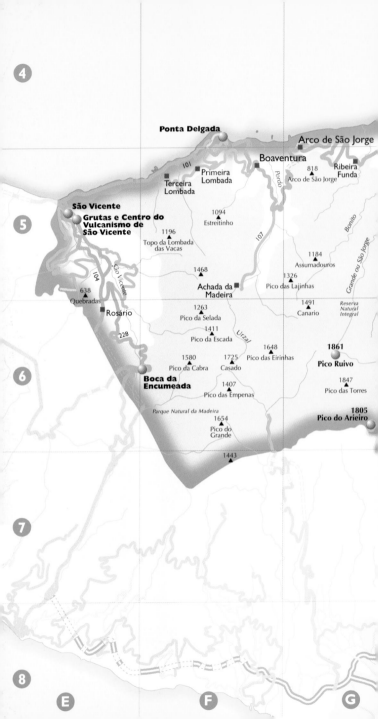

Ponta de São Jorge

■ São Jorge
507
▲ Rainha
■ Achada da Cruz
346
▲ Pinheiro
Ilha

Ilheu da Viúva ou da
Rocha do Navio

Santana
529
▲ Cortado
Ponta do Clérigo

**Parque Temático
da Madeira**
218
Faial ■
638
▲ Garajoa
981
▲ Vale da Lapa
590
▲ Penha de
Aguia
865
▲ Redondo
**Porto da
Cruz** ■
1302
▲ Pico das Pedras
494
▲ Cruzinhas
São Roque do Faial ■
1592
▲ Achada do
Teixeira
1407
▲ Chiceiros da
Queimada
Ribeira Tem-te ■
Não Caias
■ Maiada
Seca
713
▲ Pedreiro
**Ribeiro
Frio** ■
878
▲ Pico da Nogueira
1028
▲ Pico do Suna
1172
▲
1476
▲ Cabeço da Lenha
Poço do Bezerra
1306
▲ João do Prado
202
956
▲ Pico dos Porcos

Ⓗ   Ⓙ

Boca da Encumeada

HIGHLIGHTS

● Outstanding views of both the north and south coasts on clear days
● Signposted walks into the surrounding mountains

TIPS

● Be careful you don't miss the Boca da Encumeada by taking the tunnel beneath the pass instead. Coming from the north, turn off in São Vicente; coming from the south, in Serra de Água.
● The bus service is poor.

Sunny, cloud-free days are best for visiting this mountain pass where exhilarating views extend to both the north and south coasts.

Coast-to-coast vistas A halfway halt between Ribeira Brava and São Vicente, where the ER110 road meets the ER228, Boca da Encumeada is the island's lowest pass at just 1,007m (3,300ft) above sea level. Despite its modest elevation, spectacular views stretch south to the Serra de Água Valley and as far as São Vicente on Madeira's north coast—when the weather is bright and clear. On most days, however, you will find yourself climbing through fluffy cloud to reach this barren spot, then bursting through into dazzling sunlight like a passenger jet after take-off.

Views towards the jagged Serra de Água from the Boca da Encumeada, a stunning mountain pass offering some of the best views on the island and carpets of wildflowers in spring

Heading Norte The Boca da Encumeada is the starting point for a couple of dramatic cross-country walks. Extended hikes lead down to Câmara de Lobos (▷ 53) and Ribeira Brava (▷ 84), following *levadas* and tracks all the way. A more challenging marked trail (not a *levada* walk) heads east to Madeira's highest peak, Pico Ruivo (▷ 69), via Pico do Jorge (1,691m/5,548ft) and Pico das Eirinhas (1,649m/5,410ft). However, if you're just breaking your journey here, yet have a bit of time to spare (and perhaps some warm clothing, especially in winter), wander west along the Levada do Norte (Levada of the North) for a couple of kilometres; it is well worth it for the stunning views across to the south and the many wildflowers that brighten the route, particularly in spring.

THE BASICS

➕ F6
✉ On the EN104, 43km (27 miles) northwest of Funchal
🚌 6, 139
♿ None

Pico do Arieiro

TOP 25

Among the clouds on the Pico do Arieiro (left and middle); the summit (right)

THE BASICS

➕ G6

✉ 20km (12 miles) north of Funchal

🍴 Snack bar on summit

🚌 103, 138 to Poiso then hike around 6km (4 miles) to the summit

HIGHLIGHTS

● The chance to see close up the island's dramatic geology
● The stunning views across successive peaks, high above the clouds

TIPS

● Even if Funchal is scorching hot, it will be significantly cooler at the top of Pico do Arieiro, so dress accordingly.
● Come at sunrise or sunset for an even more dramatic experience.
● The walk from Pico do Arieiro to Pico Ruivo is one of the most rewarding on Madeira and is offered by many tour companies.

Drive to the top of Madeira's third-highest mountain, where panoramas of jagged, cloud-wreathed peaks will have you reaching for your camera.

Through the clouds With your own set of wheels, it's possible to drive right to the summit of the Pico do Arieiro (1,805m/5,922ft); take the EN103 via Monte to the Poiso Pass where the narrow and twisting EN202 peels off for the peak. After Poiso you'll soon find yourself above the tree line and then steering your vehicle through the clouds, at around 1,200m (3,900ft). Above the clouds, a different world opens up, one where little vegetation grows, the sun always shines and the wide-open skies are eternally blue.

Volcanic views At the top, you'll discover many have got here before you and are busy browsing the woollen stalls and drinking coffee in the snack bar. But people come for the fabulous far-reaching views across a seemingly endless parade of razor-sharp ridges, their pinnacles and peaks snagging on the cotton wool clouds. With no soil or tree cover, this is also a place where Madeira's volcanic origins are most clearly on show, with petrified lava in hues of orange, brown and purple. If you're up for more, a dramatic 6km (4-mile) trail to Pico Ruivo (▷ 69), Madeira's highest mountain, has been carved out of the mountainscape. It is tricky in places, so you'll need a head for heights and good walking boots.

TOP 25

Pico Ruivo

Top dog among Madeira's jagged pinnacles, Pico Ruivo rewards its conquerors with mountain panoramas and distant views of the island of Porto Santo on the denim-blue Atlantic.

The north face If you've not found your way to the top of Pico Ruivo (1,861m/6,106ft) on one of the long-distance footpaths, chances are you'll have made your approach from Santana, taking the lonely ER218 as far as the car park at Achada do Teixeira. From here, a rocky path climbs to the summit, steeply at first but levelling off after a while. When the path divides, take the right fork up to the rest house, where you can buy refreshments. From here, clamber to the top through the purple-hued tufas, from which the Pico Ruivo (Red Peak) takes its name, for outstanding views.

Hit the trail Two of Madeira's best mountain hikes head from the car park to other high points. An exhilarating 6km (4-mile) trail links Pico Ruivo to the summit of Madeira's third highest mountain, Pico do Arieiro (▷ 68) via tunnels, ledges cut out of vertical rock faces and vertigo-inducing ridges. The one drawback is that most large groups start the walk from Pico do Arieiro, which can make precarious passing manoeuvres on narrow paths necessary. Another demanding hike heads along a marked trail to Boca da Encumeada (▷ 66), a distance of 16km (10 miles), taking in several peaks over 1,600m (5,200ft) along the way.

THE BASICS

➕ G6
✉ 8km (5 miles) south-west of Santana
🍴 Rest house near the summit sells drinks and snacks
🚌 Taxi or private car required

HIGHLIGHT

● Far-reaching views and the considerable satisfaction of reaching the summit

TIPS

● Consider staying the night at the rest house just below the summit. This needs to be booked in advance from Funchal (tel 291 741 540); sleeping bags are not required.
● If you intend hitting the trails from Pico Ruivo, make sure you are properly equipped (▷ 11).

Ribeiro Frio

TOP
25

HIGHLIGHTS

● The views from the Balcões lookout point
● A choice of *levada* walks of varying lengths

TIPS

● If you are travelling by bus, check the schedules carefully as services here are very infrequent.
● Ribeiro Frio is chillier than the coast so bring a sweater or jacket even in summer.

Beautifully framed by wooded peaks, this isolated traveller's halt, lulled by the sounds of trickling water and the wind in the trees, is a springboard for several *levada* walks.

Halfway house Driving from Santana to Funchal, or vice versa, on the old ER103 road, Ribeiro Frio is an obvious halfway stop. The hamlet is divided into two: the lower part around the bus stop and the Faisca restaurant, and a smaller upper part where you'll find souvenir stalls and the government-owned trout farm, its circular *levada*-fed pools swirling with fish. But Ribeiro Frio's greatest attraction is its location in a deep verdant valley, at the bottom of which runs the 'cold river' from which the village takes its name.

Heavenly views from Ribeiro Frio (left) stretch all the way to the coast; this beautiful area is best explored on one of several levada *walks (right) crossing the area*

Several *levada* hikes converge in Ribeiro Frio, making it a good jumping off point for Madeira's wild interior. The most popular route is the Levada do Furado, which leads west from the upper part of the village to Portela, a distance of 12km (7 miles). Follow the path as far as the bridge across the River Bezerro (about an hour's walk) for sweeping views.

Madeira's balcony A short walk (1.5km/1 mile) out of Ribeiro Frio leads up to the Balcões (Balconies) lookout point. Take the rounded steps to the right of the Faisca restaurant, which climb high above the hamlet. At the top of the hill follow the *levada* a short way through the forest. The widescreen views, encompassing the interior's highest peaks and the distant coast, are some of the finest on the island.

THE BASICS

✚ H6
✉ 14km (9 miles) north of Funchal
🍴 Faisca (€€) near the bus stop
🚌 103, 138
♿ None

Santana

Santana's lush terraces (left) and A-frame cottages in the Parque de Temático (right)

THE BASICS

H5

⊠ 40km (25 miles) north of Funchal

🍴 Several restaurants clustered around Pico António Fernandes

🚌 103, 138

♿ Few

ℹ Sitio do Serrado, tel 291 572 992

HIGHLIGHTS

● Santana's traditional A-frame cottages
● Parque Temático da Madeira (▷ 74), an open-air museum on the edge of town devoted to Madeira's rural and craft traditions

TIPS

● If you ask politely, locals living in A-frame cottages may let you have a look around their home.
● Santana comes alive during a 24-hour folk dancing festival held in July.

A lively theme park (▷ 74) and access to the top of Madeira's highest peak draw families and hikers to this cliff-top town on the north coast. It is celebrated for its thatched A-frame cottages.

In the frame Less developed than the south, the north coast has remained true to Madeira's agricultural traditions. This can be seen in and around Santana where plum, cherry, apple and pear trees grow alongside pollarded willows and vines. The town's thatched A-frame cottages are a distinctive piece of agricultural heritage, and your first port of call should be the tourist office, housed in a perfectly renovated example. Four similar and much photographed structures stand nearby (one is a private residence), and many others in various states of repair can be spotted in and around town. Unique to Madeira, these *palheiros* first appeared in the 17th century. Used initially as houses, but later as cowsheds, they have thatched roofs reaching almost to the ground—designed to keep out the rain and wind.

Roads less travelled Climbing steeply out of Santana is the road to Achada do Teixeira (ER 218), the access point to Pico Ruivo (▷ 69). Running parallel to this, just to the north, is a steep and bumpy minor road that ends at the government mountain refuge at Queimadas. This attractive spot is the starting point for the walk along the Levada do Caldeirão Verde, one of Madeira's best hikes.

More to See

FAIAL

If you're driving along the motorway from Funchal to Santana you will pass this small hilltop village, good for a 30-minute stop. It has a pretty church and a charmingly sleepy ambience, but it is more about the views than the village itself. Faial's dramatic setting below a mammoth whaleback of rock called the Penha de Águia (Eagle Rock, 590m/1,935ft) and above a winding valley is best appreciated from the *miradouro*. Another place from which to admire the landscape is over a coffee in the small teahouse just off the small square—popular with passing tourists.

Faial's *romaria* (village festival) on 8 September brings some animation to the cobbled streets, but only fleetingly. If you are very fit, and fancy some exercise, the climb up the Penha de Águia takes around 90 minutes but the tracks are steep and rough.

J5 Casa de Chá (€) 56, 53, 78, 103, 138

GRUTAS E CENTRO DO VULCANISMO DE SÃO VICENTE

www.grutasecentrodovulcanismo.com

Created by molten lava forcing its way through joints in the rock almost 900,000 years ago (and not by the action of water erosion as is usually the case), these caves near São Vicente provide a fascinating insight into the forces that created both the island and the caves. Discovered by locals but fully explored and charted by Englishman James Johnson in the late 1880s, the 1km-long (0.6 mile) cavern wasn't opened for tourists until 1996. A 30-minute guided tour takes visitors the length of the cave, the well-informed guides bringing the imaginatively lit spaces to life. Highlights include the Lago dos Desejos (Wish Lake) and molten lava stalactites.

The tour has been extended with the construction of the Centro do Vulcanismo, where an informative audio-visual show demonstrates how Madeira was created; other

Entrance to the underworld—the caves near São Vicente

exhibits focus on volcanoes, volcanologists and the island's indigenous flora and fauna. The tour and centre make this one of the best attractions on the island and it's particularly good for kids.

➕ E5 ✉ Sítio do pé do Passo, São Vicente ☎ 291 842 404 🕓 Daily 10–7 🚌 6, 139 ♿ None 💷 Moderate

PARQUE TEMÁTICO DA MADEIRA

www.parquetematicodamadeira.pt
Spread over 7ha (17 acres) of land just off the main road through Santana, this Madeira-in-miniature is the north coast's top attraction, pitched at children and adults alike. Dotted around the park, multimedia exhibits and life-size models illustrate different aspects of Madeiran history and culture. They include ox-pulled sledges, an A-framed house, a water mill, a labyrinth, exhibits on the discovery and future of the island and much, much more. If you don't want to walk, you can get around the park on a miniature train. When the kids lose interest, there are playgrounds and grassy areas on which they can play while you retire to the (pricey) café. Perhaps the most interesting section of the park for adults is the handicrafts centre where demonstrations of traditional island skills, such as basket weaving, embroidery and pottery, take place in five small workshops.

➕ H5 ✉ Estrada Regional 101, Fonte da Pedra, Santana ☎ 291 570 410 🕓 Sep–Jun Tue–Sun 10–7; Jul–Aug daily 10–7 🍴 Café and restaurant 🚌 56, 103, 138 ♿ Very good; visitors with disabilities receive free admission 💷 Expensive

PONTA DELGADA

Just 30km (19 miles) west of Santana, and much less as the crow flies, Ponta Delgada is a remote north coast fishing village with just a couple of buses a day to the capital and a generally drowsy air. The only sight as such is the Igreja do Bom Jesus (Church of the Good Jesus), containing an 18th-century

Multimedia exhibit in the Parque Temático da Madeira

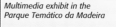

Ponta Delgada

crucifix which is the focal point of the September Festa de Senhor Jesus, one of the biggest festivals on the island. The crucifix was mysteriously washed up here in 1740 and a chapel was built to house it. When the chapel burned down in 1908 the crucifix survived, adding to its reverence. The charred cross can be seen in the church built to replace the chapel; this has a surprisingly impressive but wholly recreated baroque interior. The only other place of interest in the village is the lido which has sea pools and modern facilities.

🔹 F4 🍴 Restaurants and cafés 🚌 6

PORTO DA CRUZ

Wedged between the Penha de Águia (Eagle Rock, ▷ 73) to the north and the Pico da Coroa to the south, this tiny fishing village enjoys a spectacular location on the island's north coast. In addition to fine views, swimming in seawater pools is a big draw and great for cooling off in the summer months.

The big blank facade of the modern church is regarded as an eyesore by most visitors.

🔹 J6 🍴 Cafés and bars 🚌 Bus 53, 56, 78, 103, 138

SÃO VICENTE

At the northern end of the transisland ER104 from Ribeira Brava, São Vicente has a relaxed and prosperous air. The village started life as a fishing community by the sea, but now reaches almost 4.5km (3 miles) inland along the road. The highlight of the renovated and car-free old town is the baroque Church of St. Vincent, which has a painted ceiling depicting the saint blessing the town. Another remarkable place of worship is the seafront chapel, hollowed out of a huge boulder by local fishermen. However, the main reason for calling a halt here is to explore the Grutas e Centro do Vulcanismo de São Vicente (▷ 73).

🔹 E5 🍴 Several restaurants, cafés and bars 🚌 6, 139

The attractive village of São Vicente

A Drive around Central Madeira

This epic drive takes a whole day. It includes fishing ports, high mountain passes, verdant valleys and vertiginous sea cliffs.

DISTANCE: 120km (75 miles)   **ALLOW:** 8 hours

START

FUNCHAL
🔲 H8

1 Make an early start from Funchal to catch the fish market in Câmara de Lobos (▷ 53). From here it's a steep drive to Cabo Girão (▷ 52), some of the highest sea cliffs in Europe.

2 Continue along the coast to Ribeira Brava (▷ 84) for a dip in the sea or a drink on the renovated seafront, before exploring the delightful Igreja de São Bento.

3 Take the trans-island ER104 up to the Boca da Encumeada pass (▷ 66) where, weather permitting, you can see both the north and south coasts.

4 Point the nose of your car downwards for the descent into São Vicente (▷ 75) to visit the Grutas e Centro do Vulcanismo de São Vicente (▷ 73).

END

FUNCHAL

7 The second route to Funchal is much easier on the brakes and takes the longer but considerably faster route via Faial (▷ 73), Machico (▷ 100) and Santa Cruz (▷ 103).

6 From Santana there is a choice of two routes back to the capital—the first is a dramatic up-down traverse of the island via Ribeiro Frio (▷ 70), the Poiso Pass and Monte. A turn off at Poiso leads to the top of Pico do Arieiro (▷ 68), Madeira's third highest mountain.

5 Follow the coastline eastwards to Santana (▷ 72) for a peek into the area's typical A-frame houses and a gallivant around the Parque Temático da Madeira (▷ 74).

Restaurants

PRICES

Prices are approximate, based on a 3-course meal for one person.

€€€ over €25
€€ €15–€25
€ under €15

CANTINHO DA SERRA (€€)

Located on the Pico Ruivo road, a five-minute drive from Santana, this is a cosy inn with rustic decor, a real log fire in winter and a menu featuring hearty traditional dishes. The house specials include churrasco steak, roast goat and tenderloin with sweet potato.
H5 Estrada do Pico das Pedras, Santana 291 573 727 Tue–Sun 12.30–11

CHURRASCARIA SANTANA (€–€€)

This affordable grill restaurant in Santana attracts plenty of locals, who come for the excellent grilled meat, swordfish and tuna steaks from a succinct menu.
H5 Pico António Fernandes, Santana 291 573 879 Daily 10–10
103, 138

ESPIGA (€)

This simple café opposite the tourist office in Santana offers snacks, smiles, and seats on which to rest aching limbs after a brisk hike to Pico Ruivo. They do particularly good soups and the

pastel de nata (custard tart) is to die for.
H5 Serrado, Santana Daily 7am–8pm
103, 138

ESTRELA DO NORTE (€€)

Join the locals at this popular spot in Santana. Anything from pizza to traditional Madeiran dishes is consumed at long rows of tables in a light and airy dining room. There's a real fire on chilly northern nights.
H5 Pico António Fernandes, Santana 291 572 059 Daily 12–10
103, 138

FAISCA (€€)

Ribeiro Frio is the perfect halfway halt on the old ER103 Faial–Funchal road. This restaurant has an intimate dining room,

MADEIRAN MIXES

It seems Madeirans can distil sickly sweet liqueur from almost anything that grows on their island, with bananas, passion fruits, cherries and even fennel, chestnuts and almonds all going into the mix. *Poncha* is a very drinkable concoction of sugar-cane spirit *(aguardente)*, honey and lemon juice, while *eucolipto* is an alcoholic cold remedy made from eucalyptus seeds. Every wine shop, souvenir emporium and supermarket stocks a wide range of these potions.

a few outdoor tables with views along the valley for summer dining, and there is a good selection of Madeira classics on the menu.
H6 Ribeiro Frio 291 575 634 Daily 8am–10pm 103, 138

FERRO VELHO (€)

This popular pub in São Vicente serves hearty fish and meat dishes. Things can get lively here in the evenings when the local Coral and Zarco beers flow. Also has a pleasant garden for summer dining.
E5 Rua da Fonte Velha, São Vicente 291 842 763 Daily lunch, dinner
6, 139

O PESCADOR (€€)

This fish restaurant in Santana features new angles on traditional seafood dishes, served in a modern dining space or on the small roadside terrace. Some meat options also available.
H5 Pico António Fernandes, Santana 291 572 272 Tue–Sun noon–2am Bus 103, 138

O VIRGÍLIO (€€)

This modest place is one in a clutch of over-touted eateries on São Vicente's seafront. It serves snacks as well as full-blown meals. Free WiFi.
E5 Seafront, São Vicente 291 842 467 Daily lunch, dinner
6, 139

Western Madeira

The south coast west of Funchal catches more sunrays than anywhere else on Madeira, hence its importance to the wine and banana industries. This cannot be said of the Paúl da Serra plateau, a flat area often blanketed in fog. Cross the plateau to reach remote Porto Moniz.

Laje *Serradinho*
Seixal
Ponta do Poiso
Ilhéu das Ceroulas

▲ **Chão da Ribeira**

Reserva Natural Integral

▲ 964
Espigão

Seixal ou de Sto Antão

▲ 1445

▲ 1640
Ruivo do Paul

▲ 1375
Pico da Fajã da Lenha
▲ 1446 209
Pico da Selada

▲ 1602
Estanquinhos

110

▲ 1445

▲ 1620
Bica da Cana

▲ 418
Urze

P a ú l   d a   S e r r a

110

▲ 1415
Loiral

Parque Natural da Madeira

▲ 1512
Pedras
▲ 1368
Pico da Sra da Ajuda

105

■ **Serra de Água**

▲ 1311
Pico da Cruz ▲ 1436
Terreiros

Ponta do Sol

Santiago

209

■ Carvalhal e Carreira
■ Achada e Levada do Poiso
■ Saloes e Levada da Madelena
■ **Outeiro** **Canhas**

101

Ponta do Sol

222

Ponta do Sol

■ Lombada da Ponta do Sol
■ Candelária

Tábua

■ Furnas
■ Ribeiro da Tábua

104

Serra de Água

▲ 1155
Pico Redondo

■ Lugar da Serra

Campanário

▲ 786
Pico da Coroa
Boa Morte

Brava

Tábua

Ribeira Brava

224

Pedra de Nossa Senhora

■ **Campanário**

0 ——— 3 km
0 ——— 2 miles

D   E   F

Calheta

A quiet street in Calheta (left); looking down on the rooftops of Calheta (right)

THE BASICS

+ C7
✉ 40km (25 miles) west of Funchal
🍴 Restaurants, cafés, snack bars on the seafront and around the harbour
🚌 80, 142
♿ Few

HIGHLIGHTS

● Calheta's man-made beaches–two artificial arcs of golden sand
● Exhibitions of world-class modern art in Calheta's Centro das Artes Casa das Mudas (▷ 91)

TIP

● The best time for swimming in the sea is May–Sep. Outside these months you'll probably want to keep to the hotel pool.

Cutting-edge art, beach fun, whale-spotting and bananas galore combine to make Calheta an interesting day out. It is also a good alternative to Funchal if you have sandcastle-hungry tots in tow.

Along the prom Calheta is a tale of two towns: the seafront, backed by high, crumbling cliffs and the focal point of tourist activity, and a large settlement strung out along the valleys running inland. The long seafront promenade starts where the main road meets the sea and ends at the busy harbour, where boats depart throughout the day on fishing and wildlife-spotting trips (▷ 91). In between these are the resort's main hotel, Calheta Beach Hotel (▷ 110), the two sandy beaches as well as shops and restaurants.

Artistic heights Perched high on a cliff looking down on the seafront is the Casa das Mudas (▷ 91), one of Portugal's leading art galleries. Climbing out of town, you arrive at the parish church (Igreja Matriz da Calheta), containing a barley-twist baroque altar, rows of undulating pews and an ebony-and-silver tabernacle donated by Manuel I, King of Portugal from 1495 to 1521. Next door to the church is a sugar refinery, where you can watch rum and molasses being made. This is also the island's main banana-growing area, and large terraced plantations cover south-facing hillsides. Madeira's sweet and dinky bananas thrive on this sun-drenched southern coast.

Rocky outcrops on the northwest coast (left); the sea bathing pools at Porto Moniz (right)

Porto Moniz

This remote fishing village on the island's northwest tip is backed by almost perpendicular hills. Day-trippers come to bathe in its lava-crusted sea pools and to visit its excellent Living Science Centre.

Far-flung community This distant outpost, once several days by land from Funchal, has led a mostly sleepy existence, its hardy farmers tending slender terraces protected from the Atlantic's bluster by traditional broom fences. Whaling caused a brief flurry of activity in the mid-20th century but tourism has now become the main source of income, especially since the state-of-the-art Living Science Centre (▷ 91) opened here. Despite this, when the tour buses wheeze their way out for the long slog south to Funchal, Porto Moniz goes back to sleep.

Ocean swimming Other than the science centre, the town's chief attractions are two sets of sea pools, sculpted by volcanic activity and worn into ponds of tepid brine by millennia of wave action. When you're done with bathing, head uphill to explore the unspoilt old town. Gathered around a neatly renovated baroque church are whitewashed fishermen's cottages and an attractive town hall. If you're feeling fit, keep climbing twisting highway ER101 for dramatic views over the town and sea. Around 3km (2 miles) east of Porto Moniz the Levada da Central da Ribeira da Janela empties into the ocean. The walk along the *levada* ends near the island's only campsite (▷ 109).

THE BASICS

- ✚ C4
- ⊠ 100km (62 miles)
- 🍴 Restaurant, cafés and bars
- 🚌 80, 139
- ♿ Few

HIGHLIGHTS

- ● Natural sea pools. One of these is free to use, the other (at the western end) makes a small charge
- ● The Living Science Centre, an interactive state-of-the-art facility, ideal for children
- ● An attractive old town

TIPS

- ● Buses take 3.5 hours to reach Porto Moniz, but the scenic journey is half the pleasure.
- ● If you are driving to Porto Moniz, take the scenic south coast route there and return via the faster Paúl da Serra plateau and Boca da Encumeada (▷ 66).

Ribeira Brava

● The attractive Igreja de São Bento
● The Museu Etnográfico da Madeira, a lively presentation of Madeira's trades and crafts

● Cool off in the man-made sea pools at the western end of the promenade.
● Climb the steps at the eastern end of the promenade for the best views of the town.

A natural staging post between the northwest and Funchal, this attractive and busy resort town makes a great day trip from the capital.

Wild River Ribeira Brava translates as 'wild river' but for most of the year you would search in vain for any flowing water. Only in the winter does run-off from the mountains get funnelled along the deep valley north of the town before rushing down to the sea. Over the millennia, the river created a mini flood plain on which the town was built; settlers were attracted by a rare sight on Madeira—flat ground.

Seafront and beyond Most visitors make a beeline for the palm-lined promenade, its grey pebble beach shelving into the warm ocean.

Clockwise from far left: baroque splendour in the Igreja de São Bento; Ribeira Brava's characterful town hall; the river that gives the town its name; the seafront; view over the square on which the Igreja de São Bento stands

Strung along the promenade are numerous cafés and restaurants as well as a little round fort housing the tourist office. A short stroll behind the promenade is the town's finest piece of architecture, the Igreja de São Bento (the Church of St. Benedict). Originally built in the 15th century, it was refashioned in the baroque style in the 18th century. Its most notable feature is the chess-board tiling on the belfry roof. Inside, the chapel on the right has a Flemish painting of the Nativity encased in gilded woodwork. Some 400m (440 yards) inland, the worthwhile Museu Etnográfico da Madeira (Madeira Ethnographical Museum) occupies a renovated 19th-century sugar mill. Displays on fishing, agriculture, wine, sugar production and handicrafts include a wine press, an ox-drawn toboggan and fishing boats.

THE BASICS

✚ E8
✉ 21km (13 miles) west of Funchal
🍴 Restaurants, cafés and snack bars line the seafront
🚌 6, 7, 80 and several others
♿ Few
ℹ Forte de São Bento, tel 291 951 675
❓ The Festival of St. Peter, 29 June

Museu Etnográfico da Madeira
✉ Rua de São Francisco
☎ 291 952 598
🕐 Tue–Sun 10–12.30, 2–6
💶 Inexpensive (free on Sun)

More to See

JARDIM DO MAR

A former fishing village with some 250 inhabitants, the 'Garden of the Sea' is best known as a top surfing destination, though the beach is stony, like most beaches on the island. A leg of the World Surfing Championships takes place here every January when the waves are at their magnificent best. Away from the frothing surf, the village is delightful, a warren of cobbled lanes and alleyways radiating from a central square. Above and around the village rise terraces of banana plants, which thrive here.

🗺 B6 🍴 Cafés, bars 🚌 115, 142

PAÚL DA SERRA

Look at any map of Madeira and you will instantly recognize this large plateau, usually marked in orange, spreading over the western interior of the island. This is the Paúl da Serra, a windswept expanse of moorland measuring 17km (10 miles) by 6km (4 miles), and lying 1,300m (4,265ft) above sea level.

By far the flattest area on Madeira, the plateau was originally earmarked as the location for Madeira's international airport. However, the altitude, high winds and thick fogs that frequently smother the plateau meant the plan had to be abandoned. Instead, the area is populated by herds of cows and sheep, cropping the coarse grass and sheltering in concrete huts when the weather turns nasty. Most of the beef and lamb served in the resorts of the south coast originate on the grass-rich plateau, as does most of the island's milk. Given the choice between the mellow south coast and the wilds of the Paúl da Serra, few humans opt to live here.

🗺 D6

PONTA DO PARGO

Zarco, the explorer who discovered Madeira, is said to have caught bream off Madeira's most westerly headland, hence this village's name—'Bream Point'. Its manned

View of the Boca da Encumeada from the Paúl da Serra

lighthouse is an easy saunter west of the village, on a cliff-top perch. In the village itself, the pretty Igreja de São Pedro (Church of St. Peter) stands beside an attractive tiled fountain dating from 1899.

🚩 A5 🍴 Café-bars 🚌 80, 142

PONTA DO SOL

Just 7km (4 miles) southeast along the coast from Calheta, this small village jammed into the mouth of a river valley is worth a stop if you are passing. This stretch of the south coast gets more hours of sunlight than anywhere else on the island, hence the rows of leafy banana plants, their fruit dangling in heavy bunches. From the car park, head through the cobbled sloping streets to the baroque Igreja da Nossa Senhora da Luz (Church of Our Lady of Light) with its tiled spire and *azulejos* decoration inside. Continue further downhill to reach the short, palm-lined seafront and stony beach, continuously pounded by large waves. The village will be forever linked with the American novelist John dos Passos (1896–1970) whose grandparents were life-long residents of Ponta do Sol. A new cultural centre is named in the writer's honour (▷ 91).

🚩 D7 🍴 Restaurants, café-bars
🚌 4, 27, 80, 115, 142, 146

SEIXAL

Heaped onto a rocky headland and set against a backdrop of spectacular peaks, Seixal is an attractive halt on the precarious north coast road. If driving around the region has left you hot and sticky, its natural rock pools are a superb place in which to cool off.

In and around Seixal notice the incredibly steep vineyards, protected from the north coast's rain-laden gusts by traditional fences of heather broom. These are also set among the town's cobbled lanes, which are lined with former fishermen's cottages and a number of newer holiday homes.

✉ D5 🍴 Café-bars 🚌 139

Ponta do Sol, the sunniest spot on Madeira

Lighthouse at Ponta do Pargo, the island's western extreme

A Walk Along the Levada do Risco

Break a drive across the Paúl da Serra to explore a secret valley of ancient trees and gushing waterfalls near Rabaçal.

DISTANCE: 7km (4 miles) **ALLOW:** 2 hours 30 minutes

START

CAR PARK NEAR RABAÇAL
➕ C6

1 The start of the walk is at a car park, just outside Rabaçal, on the north side of the ER110, 17km (11 miles) west of Boca da Encumeada (▷ 66) and 22km (14 miles) east of Porto Moniz (▷ 83). (The road to Rabaçal is closed to cars, hence the need to park just off the main road.)

2 Trace the winding track downhill for 2km (1 mile) to the forestry rest house. Here you'll find toilets, picnic tables and barbecue pits.

3 Look for the sign to the right of the rest house pointing to a track to the Levada do Risco. Follow the watercourse cut into a hillside which is covered in gnarled tree heathers and huge lichens.

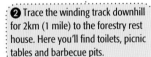

END

CAR PARK NEAR RABAÇAL

6 The only way to go now is back the way you came, but you can extend your walk by returning to the turn-off for the Levada das 25 Fontes and following that slightly more difficult path. After around 20 minutes you arrive at a lovely set of waterfalls. Again, head back the way you came and rejoin the original trail back to the car park.

5 Another 10 minutes' walk brings you to the Risco waterfall, one of the most enchanting sights on Madeira, with water gushing down the rock face into a fern-lined crater.

4 After five minutes a left fork leads to the Levada das 25 Fontes, but you should carry straight on.

A Circular Drive in the Northwest

An exhilarating circuit of the northwest with a coastal drive, a climb onto the central plateau and a long descent back into Porto Moniz.

DISTANCE: 70km (43 miles) **ALLOW:** 6 hours

START .... **END**

PORTO MONIZ
➕ C4

PORTO MONIZ

1 Start in Porto Moniz (▷ 83), at the roundabout at the mouth of the tunnel. Take the road to the nearby village of Ribeira da Janela, the location of the island's only campsite and a hydroelectric power station.

2 From Ribeira da Janela, choose between the rough and badly maintained coastal road or the new and faster tunnels.

3 Next stop Seixal (▷ 87), a great place to take a dip in the sea and have a coffee before hitting the road again.

4 From Seixal, you again have the choice between taking the tunnels, with their smooth ribbon of tarmac but no views, or a hair-raising adventure on the narrow and cliff-hugging coast road.

8 Drop down though forests and mountains to the junction with the ER101 just short of Porto Moniz.

7 Steep climbs lead up to the Paúl da Serra plateau (▷ 86), a bleak landscape of pastures and moorland often enveloped in low cloud.

6 Boca da Encumeada is an enchanting mountain pass with outstanding views of both the north and south coasts. From here stick to the ER110 heading west.

5 Around 8km (5 miles) brings you to São Vicente where the main draw is the volcanic caves (▷ 73). From here, turn inland and into the mountains. To reach the pass at Boca da Encumeada (▷ 66), turn off the ER104 onto the ER110 at Vargem.

Entertainment and Activities

CALHETA BEACHES
Madeira has only a couple of natural beaches, but the sand is of the black volcanic type. To remedy the situation, Calheta has imported sand from mainland Portugal and Morocco to create two man-made golden strands, protected from the waves by rock barriers. Both are free.
🔳 C7 ✉ Calheta seafront
🕐 Year round 🚌 80, 142

CENTRO DAS ARTES CASA DAS MUDAS
www.centrodasartes.com
Calheta's cliff-top Casa das Mudas art gallery is a must-see for anyone who likes modern art. It attracts exhibitions by world-class artists (▷ panel, this page) and incorporates a café and a gift shop.
🔳 C7 ✉ Vale dos Amores, Calheta ☎ 291 820 900
🕐 Tue–Sun 10–1, 2–6
🚌 80, 142

CENTRO CIÊNCA VIVA (LIVING SCIENCE CENTRE)
www.ccvportomoniz.com
This cutting-edge science centre near Porto Moniz has a baffling array of interactive exhibits designed to fill children (and the odd adult) with enthusiasm for science. English explanations are provided.
🔳 C4 ✉ Rotunda do Ilhéu Mole, Porto Moniz ☎ 291 850 300 🕐 Tue–Sun 10–7
🚌 80, 139

JOHN DOS PASSOS CULTURAL CENTRE
The acclaimed American writer John dos Passos was born in Chicago, but his grandparents hailed from Ponta do Sol. This cultural centre named after the village's most illustrious grandchild hosts temporary exhibitions, concerts, film screenings and other events.
🔳 D7 ✉ Rua Principe D. Luís 3, Ponta do Sol ☎ 291 974 034 🕐 Mon–Fri 9–12.30, 2–5.30 🚌 4, 27, 80, 115, 142, 146

LOBOSONDA
www.lobosonda.com
Go whale-, turtle- and dolphin-spotting off Calheta. Lobosonda organizes various trips (guaranteed to spot wildlife) and groups are small. Sunset excursions with drinks can be arranged.
🔳 C7 ✉ Harbour, Calheta ☎ 968 400 980 🕐 Sailings at 10.30, 3, weather permitting
🚌 80, 142

CLIFFHANGER
Calheta's high-tech, minimalist Casa das Mudas, designed by Madeiran-born architect Paulo David, was erected in 2004 and was nominated for the prestigious Mies van der Rohe prize in 2005.The functional and uncluttered interior has housed world-class exhibitions by Picasso and Dalí and continues to attract top-notch shows.

MADEIRA SPORTS CENTRE
www.centrodesportivoda madeira.com
Ribeira Brava is home to Madeira's largest sports complex, with a football pitch, tennis courts, sports hall, mini-golf, children's playground and more, all spread along the valley floor. Many of the facilities can be hired by the hour.
🔳 E8 ✉ Sitio da Fajã da Ribeira, Ribeira Brava ☎ 291 950 120 🕐 Daily 9–11
🚌 6, 7, 80 and others

NAUTIPOS FISHING
Boat owner Twan will take you out in the *Nautipos* for wildlife-spotting and sea fishing trips. If not out at sea with a group, he can usually be found on the harbourside.
🔳 C7 ✉ Harbour, Calheta ☎ 914 375 573 🕐 Year round 🚌 80, 142

RIBEIRA BRAVA SWIMMING COMPLEX
Ribeira Brava's indoor swimming complex and fitness centre has an adult pool with racing lanes, a kids' paddling pool and a training pool. Or you could work off all that *bolo de mel* at the fitness centre, which is equipped with treadmills and other exercise machines.
🔳 E8 ✉ Sitio dos Moinhos, Ribeira Brava ☎ 291 950 400 🕐 Mon–Fri 8–10, Sat 8–8
🚌 6, 7, 80 and others

Restaurants

WESTERN MADEIRA
RESTAURANTS

PRICES

Prices are approximate, based on a 3-course meal for one person.
€€€   over €25
€€   €15–€25
€   under €15

BORDA D'AGUA (€€)

Slightly more upmarket than the other restaurants in Ribeira Brava, Borda D'Agua serves carefully prepared seafood dishes in a smart, contemporary setting.
🔢 E8 ⊠ Rua Engeheiro Pereira Ribeiro, Ribeira Brava ☎ 291 957 697 ⏰ Daily 11–midnight 🚍 6, 7, 80 and several others

CACHALOTE (€€)

Situated on a chunk of rock among Porto Moniz's natural sea pools, this large seafood restaurant specializes in popular Madeiran classics such as rice with limpets and scabbard fish with fried banana.
🔢 C4 ⊠ Ilhéumar, Porto Moniz ☎ 291 853 180 ⏰ Daily 12–6 🚍 80, 139

DOM LUIS (€€)

This alfresco restaurant astride Ribeira Brava's promenade offers a mixed bag of decent Madeiran and international belly-fillers, mainly for ravenous tourists.
🔢 E8 ⊠ Rua Marginal da Vila, Ribeira Brava ☎ 291 952 543 ⏰ Daily 10–6 🚍 6, 7, 80 and several others

HERÉDIA (€)

A five-minute walk back from the sea, this lively café on Ribeira Brava's tiny Largo das Herédias is handy if you have a long wait for the next bus back to Funchal.
🔢 E8 ⊠ Rua São Francisco 1, Ribeira Brava ⏰ Daily 7.30am–midnight 🚍 6, 7, 80 and several others.

MAR Á VISTA (€€)

This spick-and-span seafood restaurant in Porto Moniz is a popular choice among locals and visitors alike. It enjoys lovely sea views, and an inexpensive lunch menu is available.
🔢 C4 ⊠ Porto Moniz ☎ 291 852 949 ⏰ Daily 10–10 🚍 80, 139

ONDA AZUL (€€–€€€)

The à la carte restaurant in the resort's main hotel, Calheta Beach, sports wicker chairs, crisp white linen, an outdoor terrace for summer dining, and

SEAFOOD

Menus often feature scabbard fish in many different guises, and as this monster of the deep is only caught off Madeira (and the Azores), you can rest assured it, and most other fish on the menu, hasn't been air-freighted from the other side of the globe. However, this isn't the case with *fruits de mer* (shellfish), of which hardly any originates on the island.

an international menu. Sample fare includes fillet of beef with coffee sauce, bean stew and catch of the day. Some Madeiran specialities available.
🔢 C7 ⊠ Calheta Beach Hotel, Calheta ☎ 291 820 300 ⏰ Daily 10–10.30 🚍 80, 142

ROCHA MAR (€€)

This is considered to be the best seafood restaurant in Calheta. Choose a table on the raised terrace for views of the luxury yachts moored in the marina.
🔢 C7 ⊠ Harbour road, Calheta ☎ 291 823 600 ⏰ Wed–Mon noon–1am 🚍 80, 142

SOL POENTE (€€)

High up on a rocky outcrop at the eastern end of Ponta do Sol's seafront, this snack bar provides fine sea views while you tuck into simply prepared seafood dishes, steaks or sandwiches. Good for a light lunch or early supper; there's plenty of outdoor seating.
🔢 D7 ⊠ Cais da Ponta do Sol, Ponta do Sol ☎ 291 973 579 ⏰ Daily lunch, dinner 🚍 4, 80, 115, 142, 146

VILA BALEIA (€€)

No-nonsense seafood restaurant in Porto Moniz. The emphasis here is firmly on the fish rather than the decor.
🔢 C4 ⊠ Porto Moniz ☎ 291 853 14 ⏰ Daily 10–6 🚍 80, 139

Wicker, whales and walking are the unlikely trio that make the accessible east an engaging destination. Otherwise pass beneath the struts of Madeira's airport to discover the island's second city, a statue of Christ presiding over the beach and a swimming pool at the end of a runway.

Ponta do Bode

Calhau dos
Barreiros

Ponta do
Rosto

Ilheu do
Guincho

Ponta do Castelo

Pedras Brancas
163
Ponta de São Lourenço

Estreito

214

Porta da
Abra
Ponta do
Buraco

101

214

Caniçal

Ponta das
Gaivotas

Ponta do Furado

Ilhéu da Cevada

Desembarcadouro

Ilhéu do
Farol

0   2 km

0   1 mile

L   M

Camacha

HIGHLIGHTS

● All kinds of animals crafted from wicker
● Watching the weavers at work

TIPS

● Once you've had your fill of wicker, head up to the restaurant for ocean vistas and traditional Madeiran dishes.
● Staff at O Relógio can arrange for larger wicker items to be shipped (Western Europe only) for a price.

Strong, supple and in ready supply, Madeira's wicker has been crafted into household items of all shapes and sizes for 200 years, and Camacha is the focus of this traditional industry.

The wickermen The village of Camacha has been the centre of Madeira's wicker weaving tradition since the early 19th century and, thanks in part to tourists visiting the island, this craft is still going strong. O Relógio is where it all happens; the top floor is occupied by a restaurant, but below is a multitasking wicker centre where visitors can watch weavers at work and make purchases. Most visitors head for the shop to browse the dizzying array of wicker creations. One floor down, a showroom overflows with the larger wicker designs, mostly furniture,

The whitewashed chapel of São José on Camacha's village square (left); wicker baskets piled high in the wickerwork centre of Camacha (right)

as well as a display of wicker animals and other unusual pieces. Sadly these are not for sale, no matter how much cash you stump up. The basement is where the action is, with weavers surrounded by stacks of browning willow and fresh cuttings, dexterously fashioning the sort of items you've seen upstairs.

Raw ingredients Watching Camacha's weavers work their magic is interesting, and the material they use, the willow wands, has gone through a fascinating process to reach this point. First a willow tree is felled and the thin wands that grow from the stump (called osiers) are harvested. These are boiled, stripped of their bark, left to dry then graded. The thinnest wands are transformed into baskets and newspaper racks, the thickest into tables and chairs.

THE BASICS

✚ J7
✉ 10km (6 miles) east of Funchal
☎ 291 922 114
🕐 Daily Apr–Oct 9–8.30; Nov–Mar 9–7.30
🍴 O Relógio restaurant (€€)
🚌 77, 129
♿ None
🎫 Free

Caniçal

HIGHLIGHT

● When it opens, Caniçal's new Whaling Museum is set to be the top attraction on the east coast

TIP

● A few kilometres east of Caniçal is Prainha, one of Madeira's few naturally sandy beaches.

The last port in southern Europe to cease whaling, Caniçal is reinventing itself with a new whaling museum and a chic seafront promenade.

Whaling past and present Caniçal's whaling fleet, which employed a large share of the village menfolk, was left high and dry in 1981 when an international treaty banned the catching of whales, thus saving many species from extinction. Some of the whalers assisted in the creation of a 200,000sq km (77,200sq miles) sealife refuge between Madeira and the Selvagens Islands, passing on their detailed knowledge of the area to marine biologists. For a blast from Caniçal's proud past, John Huston's1956 film *Moby Dick* includes shots of the village's whaling fleet in action.

Once an important whaling port, Caniçal has now turned to other types of fishing and to celebrating its whaling traditions in the Whaling Museum

Reinventing Caniçal Since the mid-1980s the village has been searching for a new *raison d'être*. At first the fleet turned to tuna fishing to make a living, and you'll still see plenty of boats in the harbour, but many locals are now looking towards tourism. In addition to the construction of a sleek new promenade, the Whaling Museum (Museu de Baleia) was relocated from the modest former headquarters of the Caniçal Whaling Company to a futuristic, purpose-built complex at the western end of the seafront. However, at the time of writing this had yet to open; when it does, it is sure to bristle with interactive and hands-on exhibits, and promises to be the star attraction on the east of the island. In anticipation of the influx of visitors, a couple of new restaurants have opened on Caniçal's seafront.

THE BASICS

➕ L6

✉ 32km (20 miles) east of Funchal

🍴 Restaurants, cafés along the seafront

🚌 113

Machico

HIGHLIGHTS

● Views from the top of Pico do Facho
● Man-made sandy beach and bathing facilities

TIP

● You can drive up to the top of Pico do Facho by taking a signposted turn off the main road east.

Madeira's 'second city', a small coastal town near the airport, huddles around the tight curve of the bay where man first set foot on the island.

Madeira discovered According to which story you believe, either English castaway Robert Machin or the 15th-century Portuguese navigators Zarco and Tristão Vaz Teixeira was the first person to set foot on Madeira's pebbly shore. Whoever it was, he did so here, in Machico (some say named after Machin, others after Zarco's hometown of Monchique). Zarco and Teixeira became the island's first governors in 1425, Zarco in the west and Teixeira here, in the east. A bronze statue of Teixeira stands outside the 15th-century parish church on Largo Dr. Antonío Jardim d'Oliveira.

Clockwise from left: Machico's small bay, where European discoverers first set foot; ceiling in Machico's 15th-century parish church; statue of Tristão Vaz Teixeira, one of the two people credited with discovering Madeira

Miracles and foreign sand The simple Capela dos Milagres (Chapel of Miracles) was built in 1815 to replace an earlier chapel, supposedly constructed on the site of Machin's grave. The original church had been washed into the Atlantic during a huge flood in 1803, but its Gothic crucifix was found floating out at sea by an American sailor. 'Miracle!' cried locals, and have celebrated the event every year since. Just back from Machico's elegant promenade stands the triangular, ochre-coloured Forte de Nossa Senhora do Amparo, built in 1706 to ward off pirate attacks; it now houses the tourist office. A short walk east is the town's new public beach, its golden sand imported from Morocco. Rising above the marina is the 320m-high (1,050ft) Pico do Facho (Peak of the Torch), which has views of planes gliding into the nearby airport.

THE BASICS

🞣 K7
✉ 24km (15 miles) north-east of Funchal
🍴 Cafés and restaurants in Rua do Mercado
🚌 20, 53, 60, 103, 156 and Machico express
ℹ Forte Nossa Senhora do Amparo, tel 291 962 289
❓ Machico celebrates the discovery of Madeira on 1 July, Gastronomy Week in early August, the Miraculous Crucifix Procession on 8 October

Forte de Nossa Senhora do Amparo
☎ 291 962 289
🕐 Mon–Fri 9–5, Sat 9–noon
♿ None
🎫 Free

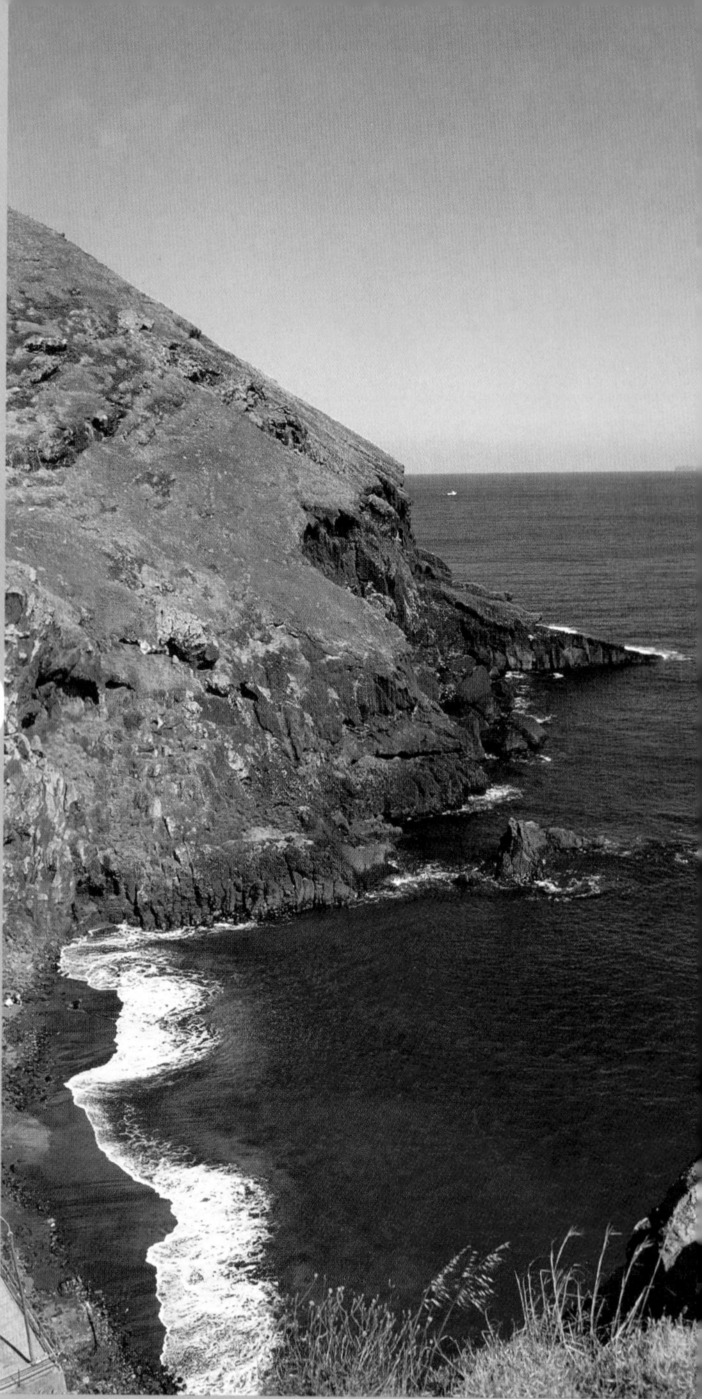

GARAJAU

A few years ago the only reason to stop off at this wind-lashed promontory was to stare up at the impressive, late-1920s statue of Jesus Christ on the cliff top, arms outspread and gazing out to sea. However, recently, the grey-pebble beach below the cliff has been developed, with a café, changing facilities and even a cable car for bathers' convenience.

➕ H8 🍴 Seasonal café 🚌 2, 109, 110, 155, 136 to Caniço

PONTA DE SÃO LOURENÇO

Like the wake left by a ship, the Ponta de São Lourenço trails behind the rest of the island, forming its most easterly point. In sharp contrast to the lushness of the interior, the starkly beautiful landscape is reminiscent of Porto Santo. There is an easy 3.5km (2 mile) walk from the bus stop at Baía d'Abra almost to the end of the peninsula, passing towers of rock marooned offshore and striated cliffs. It isn't possible to reach the very end of the peninsula as it breaks up into islands two-thirds of the way along. On the last of these islands a lighthouse keeps fog-bound fishing boats away from the rocks. If you are tackling the walk in summer, bring a hat and plenty of water as there is no shade on the peninsula.

➕ L6 🍴 Snack bar at Baía d'Abra 🚌 113 to Baía d'Abra

SANTA CRUZ

This is the nearest town to Santa Caterina Airport; its houses begin just 200m (220 yards) from the southern end of the runway. It has a long pebbly seafront and a lido, from which you can watch jets landing and taking off. In town is the whitewashed Igreja de Santa Cruz, a pretty church sporting simple Manueline embellishments. Just west of the town, the Aquaparque offers various giant slides and pools and a 'lazy river' (▷ 105).

➕ K7 🍴 Numerous restaurants, cafés and bars 🚌 20, 23, 53, 113, 156

The rugged coast of Ponta de São Lourenço, the island's most easterly point (opposite); the 19th-century law courts in Santa Cruz (above)

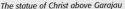

The statue of Christ above Garajau

A Drive Around
Eastern Madeira

This half-day spin around Madeira's eastern extremities takes in beautiful gardens, a sandy beach and the island's second 'city'.

DISTANCE: 60km (37 miles) **ALLOW:** 6 hours

START **END**

FUNCHAL
➕ H8

GARAJAU
➕ H8

❶ Head east from Funchal on the south coast motorway and take the exit marked Camacha.

❽ The last stop is Garajau (▷ 103) overlooked by a statue of Christ, a mini version of the Rio statue.

❷ After 2km (1 mile) a turn to the right leads to the Jardins do Palheiro (▷ 60), once the home of the Blandy family of wine merchants.

❼ Returning to Funchal, the motorway passes under Madeira International Airport, emerging at Santa Cruz (▷ 103). Stop here for a refreshing swim at the lido and watch jets approaching the runway less that 500m (550 yards) away.

❸ Head back to the ER102 and drive north to Camacha (▷ 96) for a wander around the wicker workshop in O Relógio, followed by a coffee in the restaurant upstairs.

❻ From Machico, take the motorway north, skirt around Caniçal and keep going until the road runs out. This is the Ponta de São Lourenço (▷ 103), a snaking peninsula ending at a lighthouse.

❹ From Camacha stick to the ER102 until you reach Santo António da Serra. Here you'll discover the undervisited Quinta da Serra, home to the Blandy family of wine merchants before they moved to the Palheiro Gardens.

❺ Take the ER207 towards the airport to rejoin the motorway for the short drive to Machico (▷ 100), where there's a new man-made beach.

DRIVE

EASTERN MADEIRA

Shopping

O BALEIRO & LOJA MOBY DICK
There may not be a whole lot of Caniçal's whaling past to see these days, but these two kiosks specialize in whale bone and other whale-related mementos.
➕ L6 ✉ Seafront, Caniçal
🚌 113

CASA DAS BORDADEIRAS
Some of the best embroidery comes from Machico. Watch it being made at this shop-cum-workshop on the highway through town.
➕ K7 ✉ Sitio da Pontinha, Machico ☎ 291 966 655
🚌 Machico express, 20, 53, 60, 103, 156

O RELÓGIO
This shop has everything you ever wanted—but in wicker. Pile upon pile of baskets, trays, chairs, tables, magazine racks and countless other items. (▷ 96).
➕ J7 ✉ Largo da Achada, Camacha ☎ 291 922 114
🚌 77, 110, 129

THE WINE SHOP
An atmospheric and aromatic wine store with a large assortment of Madeiras and inter-national spirits. This is one of Machico's oldest shops, owned by genera-tions of the same family.
➕ K7 ✉ Rua da General António Teixeira de Aguiar 52, Machico ☎ 291 962 599
🚌 Machico express, 20, 53, 60, 103, 156

Entertainment and Activities

AQUAPARQUE SANTA CRUZ
www.aquaparque.com
Madeira's only water park has five toboggan rides, four fast slides, two pools and paddling areas. In a valley at the southern end of the village.
➕ K7 ✉ Ribeira da Boaventura, Santa Cruz
🕐 Daily 10–6 🚌 20, 23, 53, 113, 156

LA BARCA DISCOTHEQUE
www.discotecalabarca.com
The epicentre of Machico's tiny nightlife scene, La Barca holds regular event nights, often going on until dawn. Retro-trendy interior; pool tables too.
➕ K7 ✉ Praceta 25 de Abril, Machico ☎ 968 073 991 🕐 Daily 11pm–3am
🚌 Machico express, 20, 53, 60, 103, 156

COMPLEXO BALNEAR DO CANIÇAL
Modern swimming complex in Caniçal with

> ### GOING TO EXTREMES
> With so many mountains, valleys, sheer drops and rivers, Madeira is ideal for canyoning, hang-gliding mountain biking and climb-ing. Local adventure sports company Terras de Aventura (Caminho do Amparo, 25, Funchal, tel 291 708 990; www.terrasdeaventura.com) can help you get tooled up and off the ground.

two pools and access to the sea.
➕ L6 ✉ Seafront, Caniçal
🕐 Summer only 🚌 113

DIVING CENTRE BALEIA
Courses and dives for novices and more experi-enced divers.
➕ K7 ✉ Hotel Dom Pedro, Machico ☎ 91 967 435
🚌 Machico express, 20, 53, 60, 103, 156

FORUM MACHICO
Large modern arts com-plex overlooking the bay. Facilities include an auditorium, a library and a cinema.
➕ K7 ✉ Promenade, Machico ☎ 291 969 370
🚌 Machico express, 20, 53, 60, 103, 156

Restaurants

A BRISA DO MAR (€€)

The restaurant-cum-café located inside Caniçal's swimming complex does a superb line in seafood and grilled meat for hungry bathers.

✚ L6 ✉ Complexo Balnear do Caniçal, Caniçal ☎ 291 960 726 🕐 Daily 10–midnight 🚌 113

CABRESTANTE (€€)

Enjoy a coffee break downstairs in the café, or make a meal of it in the fancier dining room upstairs. The chef's specialities at this seafront restaurant include fish pie and spaghetti with *fruits de mer*.

✚ L6 ✉ Sítio Palmeira Baixo, Caniçal ☎ 291 960 000 🕐 Wed–Mon 11–11 🚌 113

CASA DE CHÁ (€)

Attractive new tea rooms in the rejuvenated grounds of Machico's Museu Municipal. Offers 35 types of tea and a selection of simple snacks, in an up-to-the-minute setting.

✚ K7 ✉ Museum, Rua do Ribeirinho, Machico 🕐 Daily 9.30–8 🚌 Machico express, 20, 53, 60, 103, 156

O GALÃ (€–€€)

This down-to-earth snack bar in Machico is the locals' choice for cheap and filling fare, including fish dishes, barbecued meat, pizzas, burgers and sandwiches.

✚ K7 ✉ Rua da General António Teixeira de Aguiar 3, Machico ☎ 291 965 720 🕐 Daily 8am–10pm 🚌 Machico express, 20, 53, 60, 103, 156

GONÇALVES (€€)

Feast on fish, meat and inexpensive specials at this appealingly modern place near the Forum Machico. If you've never tried wreckfish (a large bass-like fish), now is the time.

✚ K7 ✉ Rua do Ribeirinho, Machico ☎ 291 966 606 🕐 Daily 8–11 🚌 Machico express, 20, 53, 60, 103, 156

SOMETHING FRUITY

Custard apples, papayas, passion fruits, guavas, mangoes, avocados, bananas, cherries, apples, pears—the list of subtropical fruits cultivated on Madeira could go on. Thanks to the fertile volcanic soil and the year-round mild climate Funchal's *mercado* overflows with fruit 365 days of the year. It is a popular dessert and some fruits are used in savoury dishes. In supermarkets, 'Country of Origin Portugal' often means the produce comes from Madeira.

MERCADO VELHO (€€)

A delightful place in Machico's old municipal market. The indoor dining room has quite an upmarket vibe while outside tables cluster around the old fountain where market traders once sold their wares.

✚ K7 ✉ Mercado Velho, Machico ☎ 291 965 926 🕐 Daily 10–midnight 🚌 Machico express, 20, 53, 60, 103, 156

O PESCADOR (€€–€€€)

Just off Machico's beach, this bright fish restaurant has a stunning, clean-cut interior as well as a more relaxed terrace that's perfect for lunch. The menu is packed with local seafood, but if fish is not your thing retreat to the basement pizzeria.

✚ K7 ✉ Frente á Praia de Areia Amarela, Machico ☎ 291 966 022 🕐 Daily noon–late 🚌 Machico express, 20, 53, 60, 103, 156

O RELÓGIO (€€)

On Camacha's main square, this is the hub of the wicker industry. Upstairs, the large and traditional restaurant offers a welcome retreat from wicker frenzy. Has ocean views and fish, meat and pasta dishes are served.

✚ J7 ✉ Largo da Achada, Camacha ☎ 291 922 114 🕐 Daily lunch, dinner 🚌 77, 110, 129

Madeira offers an excellent range of accommodation, from luxurious *quintas* set in extensive grounds to small hotels in the city centre or family resorts.

Introduction

Most visitors stay in large four- and five-star hotel complexes in the 'hotel zone' west of Funchal city centre. For those on tighter budgets, renting an apartment works out good value, as do local guesthouses.

Madeira

The overwhelming majority of Madeira's hotels are strung along the Avenida do Infante and Estrada Monumental, leading from the Rotunda do Infante near the tourist office to Praia Formosa, 4.5km (3 miles) to the west. This main artery bustles from dawn until late evening with tour buses, 4X4s departing and returning from trips, and Funchal's yellow buses.

Alternatives to the hotel zone include the city centre, where you'll find guesthouses and design hotels, and out-of-town mansions *(quintas)* that have been converted into accommodation. Apart from Funchal, there's a large concentration of luxury resorts around Caniço, just east of Funchal, and Machico, Calheta and several other coastal towns have good accommodation. For a completely different experience, stay in the mountainous interior, the ideal location if you want to conquer a few *levadas*.

Porto Santo

With its 7km (4-mile) sandy beach, the island of Porto Santo has low-rise luxury resorts along the southern shore, where the emphasis is on relaxation, sport and beach fun. Porto Santo fills quickly in July and August, making advance booking essential.

APARTMENTS AND APARTHOTELS

An excellent way to save on the cost of accommodation and of meals out in restaurants is to rent a holiday apartment or a room with kitchenette in an 'aparthotel'. Madeira has a lot of this type of accommodation, mostly in the three- and four-star categories. A good place to begin researching options is Madeira Apartments (www.madeiraapartments.com), a reliable agency dealing with a range of places, from budget to luxury.

From top: The Vine, Funchal; Windsor, Funchal; Porto Santa Maria, Funchal; Quinta do Serrado, Porto Santo; Quinta Splendida, Caniço

Budget Hotels

ESTALAGEM EIRA DO SERRADO

www.eiradoserrado.com
If you're planning to do some walking and want to stay in the countryside, this modern complex near the lookout point above Curral das Freiras is a comfortable choice. Rooms are generously cut, and the mountain views are mesmerizing.

➕ F7 ✉ Eira do Serrado, Curral das Freiras
☎ 291 724 220 🚌 81

EURO MONIZ

www.euromoniz.com
Staying in Porto Moniz, two hours' drive from Funchal, may not be for everyone, but the 40 comfortable rooms, indoor swimming pool and low prices at this hotel may make the idea more appealing.

➕ C4 ✉ Porto Moniz
☎ 291 850 050 🚌 80, 139

ORCA PRAIA

www.orcapraia.com
Right at the top of the budget price range, this 128-room resort is bolted onto the side of a cliff 6km (4 miles) west of Funchal city centre. It has an outstanding pool, and all rooms have large balconies with stunning ocean views.

➕ G8 ✉ Estrada Monumental 355, Funchal
☎ 291 707 070

ORQUÍDEA

www.hotel-orquidea.com
Tucked away in a Funchal backstreet, the 'Orchid' is a plush place for this price bracket. Has views of the cathedral and the sea from the roof terrace, a good restaurant and courteous staff.

➕ b1 ✉ Rua dos Netos 69–71, Funchal
☎ 291 200 120

RESIDENCIAL SANTA CLARA

This 14-room guesthouse just past the Convent of St Clara provides old-fashioned accommodation for those who don't mind trading mod-cons for local character.

➕ G8 ✉ Calçada do Pico 16 B, Funchal ☎ 291 742 194

RESIDENCIAL ZARCO

www.residencialzarco.com
The central location, on a pocket-sized square just off Funchal's Avenida do Mar, is second to none. The staff are obliging and the rooms are clean, but no one could accuse this place of being overly smart. A good choice for backpackers who are on a tight budget.

➕ c2 ✉ Rua da Alfândega 113, Funchal ☎ 291 223 716

VILA LUSITÂNIA

www.vila-lusitania.com
Located around 500m (550 yards) north of Funchal's Lido, this villa guesthouse combines good facilities and excellent service. The 26 en-suite rooms are clean and attractive, and many have balconies and ocean views. The pool is a big draw, as hotels with pools in the budget price category are rare.

➕ G8 ✉ Rua Fundação Cecília Zino 26, Funchal
☎ 291 773 603 🚌 48

WINDSOR

www.hotelwindsorgroup.pt
This medium-sized hotel (67 rooms) has a rooftop swimming pool, smart restaurant, comfortable, well-equipped rooms and a private car park. One of three hotels in Funchal belonging to the Windsor group, it is worth every euro. Most of the rooms face into a courtyard.

➕ c2 ✉ Rua das Hortas 4C, Funchal ☎ 291 233 081

WHERE TO STAY BUDGET HOTELS

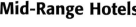

Mid-Range Hotels

PRICES

Expect to pay €75–€150 per night for a double room in a mid-range hotel.

CALHETA BEACH HOTEL

www.hotelcalhetabeach.com
Dominating Calheta's promenade, this is a large resort-style hotel, but it displays creative touches and imaginative colour schemes, and has a first-rate restaurant, Onda Azul (▷ 92). The resort has two sandy beaches.
➕ C7 ✉ Seafront, Calheta ☎ 291 820 300 🚌 80, 142

O COLMO

www.hotelocolmo.com
The main hotel in Santana, this is a good choice if you're looking for a base in the countryside. It has a superb restaurant, comfortable, if unexciting, rooms, and is on the main drag.
➕ H5 ✉ Sítio do Serrado, Santana ☎ 291 570 290 🚌 103, 138

DOM PEDRO

www.dompedrobaiahotel.com
The place to stay in Machico, Dom Pedro has comfortable rooms, a tennis court, diving centre and restaurant. The beach is a five-minute walk along the promenade.
➕ K7 ✉ Estrada de São Roque, Machico ☎ 291 724 215 🚌 20, 53, 60, 103, 156 and Machico express

FOUR VIEWS MONUMENTAL LIDO

www.monumentallido madeira.com
This very conspicuous hotel on the main road through Funchal's hotel zone just scrapes into the mid-range category. Popular with families, it offers great value, especially the rooms with sea views. It's a short hop by bus to the sights of Funchal.
➕ G8 ✉ Estrada Monumental 284, Funchal ☎ 291 724 000 🚌 1, 2, 4, 6, 12

FUNCHAL DESIGN HOTEL

www.funchaldesignhotel.com
This is a funky new design hotel in the very heart of Funchal. Rooms have big print wallpaper, internet access, sound system, state-of-the-art

THE QUINTA

The word *quinta* best translates as 'mansion'. These mini-stately homes, built by wealthy sugar and wine merchants in the 18th and 19th centuries, once hosted aristocratic visitors on extended sojourns to the island. Many of them have been converted into hotels representing a characterful alternative to the hotel zone's glass and concrete. The best *quintas* have antique furniture, tropical gardens and serene out-of-town settings

showers, and bathrobes are provided.
➕ G8 ✉ Rua da Alegria 2, Funchal ☎ 291 201 800

HOTEL DO CAMPO

www.hoteldocampo.com
Arguably the best hotel in Ribeira Brava and just a pebble's throw from the sea. The communal areas are light and airy, the rooms comfortable and well kitted out, and the pool is a godsend after a day on the *levadas*.
➕ E8 ✉ Estrada da Banda de Além 25, Ribeira Brava ☎ 291 950 270 🚌 6, 7, 80 and several others

MELIÃ MADEIRA MARE

www.meliamadeiramare.com
Check into this 220-room resort for classy accommodation, probably the best-equipped spa on the island, a fabulous pool and five restaurants. The rooms are spacious with their own balcony, and mostly with sea views.
➕ G8 ✉ Rua Leichlingen 2–4, Funchal ☎ 291 773 617 🚌 1, 2, 4, 6, 12

PORTO SANTA MARIA

www.portobay.com
A location in the Zona Velha, first-class facilities, reasonable rates and rooms with grandstand views of the harbour make this one of the best places to lay your head in Funchal. Also has large indoor and outdoor pools.
➕ e3 ✉ Avenida do Mar 50, Funchal ☎ 291 206 700

QUINTA BELA SÃO TIAGO

www.quintabelasaotiago.com
Something of a well-kept secret, this manor house just outside Funchal's Zona Velha, was the residence of the island's vice-governor before it was turned into a hotel. The rooms are beautifully furnished and facilities include a heated pool set in stunning gardens, and free WiFi on the terraces.

➕ e2 ✉ Rua Bela de São Tiago, Funchal ☎ 291 724 233

QUINTA DO ESTREITO

www.quintadoestreitomadeira.com
The rooms at this traditional mansion set in tropical gardens are brochure-perfect with appealing colour schemes and simple, antique-style furnishings. It's a 15-minute drive from Funchal, but there's a free twice-daily shuttle bus to the city.

➕ F8 ✉ Rua José Joaquim da Costa, Estreito de Câmara de Lobos ☎ 291 910 530
🚌 3, 137

QUINTA PERESTRELLO

www.quintaperestrellomadeira.com
An old mansion with a modern annex, this intimate hotel is not quite the full-scale *quinta* experience, but it has restful gardens, 36 well-furnished rooms and a secluded pool.

➕ G8 ✉ Rua Dr. Pita 3, Funchal ☎ 291 724 237
🚌 1, 2, 4, 6, 12

QUINTA DAS VISTAS

www.quintadasvistasmadeira.com
As the name suggests, the wow factor is provided by the views across Funchal. Rooms are studies in elegance, service impeccable, and there's free Wi-Fi in the rooms.

➕ G8 ✉ Caminho de Santo António 52, Funchal ☎ 291 750 007

QUINTA DO SERRADO

www.quintadoserrado.com
Located on a grassy slope on the north side of Porto Santo, this stone-built low-rise complex is a great rural retreat. Rooms are attractive, and the list of facilities means you'll never have to leave the building, except, perhaps to cycle to the beach.

➕ BI ✉ Sitio do Pedregal, Porto Santo ☎ 291 980 270

CHANGING SEASONS

Room rates are highest in the European holiday months of July and August and around Christmas and New Year, and lowest in November and January through to March. Rates can spike around the Flower Festival (Apr), Carnival (Feb) and Easter. Funchal's luxury hotels offer the best bargains off season.

ROCA MAR

www.hotelrocamar.com
Located as near to the cliff edge as the architects dared, two-thirds of the rooms at this well-appointed resort hotel have sea views. The swimming pool is encased in a 'lightning flash' of concrete that extends out into the Atlantic.

➕ J8 ✉ Caminho Cais da Oliveira, Caniço ☎ 291 934 334 🚌 2, 109, 110, 155, 136

SPORT HOTEL GALOSOL

www.galoresort.com
This cliff-top hotel in Caniço has bright rooms, indoor and outdoor pools, a spa and wellness centre, a range of sports activities and outstanding sea views. It also has a private concrete-and-rock beach complex.

➕ J8 ✉ Rua D. Francisco Santana 12, Caniço
☎ 291 930 934 🚌 2, 109, 110, 155, 136

THE VINE

www.hotelthevine.com
Prices at Madeira's most exciting design hotel are just low enough to dip into the mid-range bracket, and if you appreciate contemporary flair, you won't regret staying here. Sleekly furnished rooms, a luxurious spa, a panoramic restaurant and a magnificent rooftop pool make for a very glamorous experience.

➕ a2 ✉ Rua dos Aranhas 27, Funchal ☎ 291 009 000

Luxury Hotels

PRICES

Expect to pay over €150 per night for a double room in a luxury hotel.

CHOUPANA HILLS

www.choupanahills.com
Repeatedly nominated as one of the world's best resort hotels, Funchal's Choupana Hills has stylish rooms in wooden bungalows dotted over a leafy hillside with views of the city. Facilities include two pools, a spa and a tea lounge.

➕ H8 ✉ Travessa do Largo da Choupana, Funchal ☎ 291 206 020

PESTANA PORTO SANTO

www.pestana-porto-santo.com
A wonderful low-rise resort just behind Porto Santo's golden beach. Rooms are a little snug, but tastefully furnished and some have balconies with sea views. Closed in winter.

➕ BII ✉ Estrada Regional 111, 120, Sítio do Campo de Baixo, Porto Santo
☎ 291 144 000

QUINTA DA CASA BRANCA

www.quintacasabranca.pt
Despite its rather functional, modern appearance—not what you would expect from a *quinta*—this hotel just north of Funchal's hotel zone has many loyal fans. It is peaceful, tastefully designed and the staff are solicitous; you won't want to leave.

➕ G8 ✉ Rua da Casa Branca 7, Funchal ☎ 291 700 770

QUINTA DO MONTE

www.quintadomontemadeira.com
Secluded, well-appointed *quinta* in Monte, just outside Funchal. Has elegant public spaces furnished with antiques, comfortable rooms and an indoor pool. The restaurant (▷ 62) is one of the best on the island.

➕ H8 ✉ Caminho do Monte 192/194, Monte ☎ 291 724 236 🚌 20, 21, 48

QUINTA SPLENDIDA

www.quintasplendida.com
The aptly named Splendida is a stunning spa resort set in extensive gardens in Caniço, east of Funchal. Some accommodation is in self-contained bungalows. There's a spa, with an indoor pool, plus an outdoor one to die for.

➕ J8 ✉ Estrada Ponta da Oliveira 11, Caniço ☎ 291 930 401 🚌 2, 109, 110, 155, 136

REID'S PALACE

www.reidspalace.com
Follow in the footsteps of Winston Churchill, Fidel Castro and King Edward VIII at Funchal's most famous hotel. Established in 1891 (▷ panel, this page), it blends understated elegance with great facilities.

➕ G8 ✉ Estrada Monumental 139, Funchal ☎ 291 717 171 🚌 1, 2, 4, 6, 12

SAVOY RESORT

www.savoyresort.com
Comprising three hotels (Classic, Royal and Gardens), this is possibly Madeira's most luxurious hotel. It has a great location, within ambling distance of Funchal city centre. Visitors have included Ronaldo and the King of Spain.

➕ G8 ✉ Rua Carvalho Araújo, Funchal ☎ 291 213 000/500/600

TIVOLI MADEIRA

www.tivolihotels.com
Near Funchal's Lido, this member of a Portuguese chain has 317 immaculate rooms, all with a sea-facing balcony. Offers a spa, pool and any service you could imagine.

➕ G8 ✉ Rua Simplício dos Passos Gouveia 29, Funchal ☎ 291 702 000

THE BIRTH OF REID'S

The son of a poor Scottish crofter, William Reid ran away to sea in 1836 and eventually washed up on Madeira. He began a business renting out *quintas* to wealthy Europeans and then commissioned the building of a luxury hotel. Unfortunately, he died in 1888 before Reid's Palace was finished. The hotel eventually opened in 1891 and remains *the* place to stay on Madeira.

This section is full of practical information on planning a trip to Madeira, and finding your way around once you're there. It includes language tips and historical pointers.

Planning Ahead

When to Go

Madeira is a popular winter sun destination for Europeans escaping the northern winter, while the Portuguese arrive en masse in July and August, fleeing the mainland's stifling heat. If you prefer to travel at quieter times, November, January and most of February are best.

<table>
TIME

L Same as UK and Portugal—GMT, with daylight saving April to October; one hour behind most of mainland Europe.
</table>

AVERAGE DAILY MAXIMUM TEMPERATURES

JAN	FEB	MAR	APR	MAY	JUN	JUL	AUG	SEP	OCT	NOV	DEC
64°F	66°F	66°F	68°F	70°F	72°F	75°F	77°F	77°F	73°F	72°F	66°F
18°C	19°C	19°C	20°C	21°C	22°C	24°C	25°C	25°C	23°C	22°C	19°C

Spring (March to May) is mild, sunny but cool with the occasional rainy day.
Summer (June to August) is normally hot and sunny but the heat is moderated by Atlantic winds. Temperatures rise to around 25°C (77°F).
Autumn (September to October) is dry and sunny with temperatures gradually falling from their summer highs.
Winter (November to February) brings a mixed bag of sunny days, grey misty periods and occasionally heavy rain. Temperatures rarely fall below 17°C (63°F).

WHAT'S ON

January *Grand New Year Firework Show* (midnight 31 Jan): Biggest firework display in the world; *Madeira Walking Festival* (late Jan): Hundreds of walkers converge on 20 of the best trails, over five days.
February *Carnival* (fortnight leading up to Shrove Tuesday): Costumed parades and samba across the island.
March *Madeira Island Open Golf Tournament* (late Mar): Madeira's premier golf event held at the Santo da Serra course.
April *Flower Festival* (second or third weekend): Flower displays and folk events around Funchal.
June *Atlantic Festival* (throughout Jun): Music, fireworks and a multitude of cultural events in Funchal; *Madeira Rally* (variable dates): Classic car rally.
July *Funchal Jazz Festival* (first week Jul): Popular jazz festival; *Machico Food Festival* (late Jul): Festival in Machico celebrating the island's gastronomy.
August *Feast of the Assumption* (15 Aug): Celebrated with particular verve in Monte, with religious processions and partying come darkness; *Madeira Wine Rally* (variable dates): International rally around the island.
September *Madeira Wine Festival* (early Sep): Held in Câmara de Lobos; *Columbus Festival* (early Sep): Biggest annual event on Porto Santo.
November *Festa da Castanha* (1 Nov): Chestnut Festival in Curral das Freiras.
December *Advent and Christmas celebrations*: Elaborate Nativity scenes, street illuminations, Christmas trees and church services.

Madeira Online

www.madeiratourism.org
The official tourist board website is a good place to start finding out about Madeira.

www.madeira-web.com
Very informative website belonging to the Strawberry World Group. Some of the information needs updating but generally good.

www.madeira-live.com
Webcams, videos, photos and lots more provided by online magazine dedicated to Madeira.

www.museumac.com
An interesting virtual project on the museums of Madeira, the Azores and the Canary Islands and examining the cultural traits that link them.

www.themadeiratimes.com
An online newspaper and guide for expats and tourists. The forum is particularly useful if you're looking to buy property on Madeira.

www.madeirawineguide.com
A non-commercial site with information on everything you ever wanted to know about Madeira wine, from the history of its production to how to re-cork vintages.

www.madeiraonline.com
Lists businesses, tourist sites, government offices and much more.

www.madeiranature.com
Website of an organization promoting nature tourism on Madeira. The emphasis is on eco-tourism and the island's protected areas.

www.madeirarural.com
Website belonging to a non-profit association promoting all kinds of rural accommodation from rural hotels and *quintas* to self-catering cottages and bed-and-breakfasts.

WIFI

WiFi Madeira (www.wifi-madeira.com) is a free internet service available on seafronts and major squares in 11 towns across the island. However, although you'll have few problems getting connected in Funchal, outside the capital the service is poorly maintained and unreliable. Most resorts and aparthotels offer WiFi, free to guests but for a fee to non-residents. If all else fails, McDonald's on Funchal's Avenida do Mar provides free WiFi for customers.

INTERNET CAFÉS

Insularmatica Cyber Café
🔁 d2
✉ C.C. Anadia, unit 38-40, Funchal
☎ 291 233 770
🕐 Daily 10–10

Cremesoda
🔁 b1
✉ Rua dos Ferreiros 9, Funchal
☎ 291 224 920
🕐 Daily 10–10

Getting There

INSURANCE

EU nationals are entitled to emergency medical treatment on presentation of a European Health Insurance Card (EHIC). Obtain one before travelling: the fastest method is to apply online at www.ehic.org.uk (UK citizens) or www.ehic.ie (Irish citizens). US visitors should check their health insurance cover before departure. In all cases full travel insurance is advisable, particularly if your household insurance doesn't cover the items you're taking with you. In the unlikely event that any of your possessions are stolen, you should obtain a police report for your insurance company. Hotels should be able to provide an interpreter.

TOURIST INFORMATION

● Madeira Tourist Board: www.madeiratourism.org
● Portuguese tourist offices:
UK, tel 020 7201 6666
USA, tel 646 723 0200
Ireland, tel 0167 091 33
Germany, tel 302 541 060
Sweden, tel 0850 652 100

AIRPORTS

Madeira International Airport (FNC) is 18km (11 miles) east of Funchal. Porto Santo airport (PXO) extends north–south across Madeira's 'other' island.

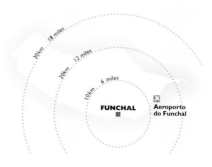

30km / 18 miles
20km / 12 miles
10km / 6 miles
FUNCHAL
Aeroporto do Funchal

ARRIVING BY AIR

Madeira airport, often still called Santa Catarina or just Funchal airport (tel 291 520 700; www. anam.pt) is within easy striking distance of Funchal and most of the rest of the island. It lies just 3km (2 miles) from Machico but over 120km (75 miles) from Porto Moniz (all distances by road).

If you are staying at one of the large hotels in the hotel zone, you will be met by a representative at arrivals. Some small guesthouses and apartment landlords also offer this service. Otherwise the airport bus (€5) operated by SAM runs every 45 minutes from 9.45am to 9.15pm from outside arrivals to the hotel zone (45 minutes) via Funchal city centre. Many other public buses stop at the airport, but these terminate in central Funchal.

Taxis wait at the rank outside the arrivals hall. A typical fare from the airport to Funchal is between €25 and €35.

Car hire companies with desks at the airport include Avis (tel 291 524 392; www.avis.com. pt), Auto Jardim (tel 291 524 023; www.auto-jardim.com), Europcar (tel 291 524 633; www.

europcar.pt) and Rodavante (tel 291 524 718; www.rodavante.com). Note that other local hire companies do not have airport desks. If you have booked ahead with one of these companies, you will be met by a representative who will take you to the company's depot.

ARRIVING BY SEA
Funchal is an increasingly popular port of call for cruise ships belonging to Thomas Cook, MSC and P&O. Cruise passengers disembark at the harbour, where coaches transport them to the sights and activities across the island, such as Funchal's markets, the Botanical Gardens, Monte and Câmara de Lobos. Central Funchal is a 15-minute walk from the quay.

TRAVEL BETWEEN MADEIRA AND PORTO SANTO
Up to four flights a day, operated by an Azorean airline called SATA (www.sata.pt), link Madeira with Porto Santo. The flight time is a mere 20 minutes and fares are reasonable. Porto Santo Airport (tel 291 980 120; www.anam.pt) stretches almost from one side of the island to the other. Taxis wait outside the small terminal and the highest fare you can pay is €13.

Car hire companies on Porto Santo include Rodavante (tel 291 982 925), Auto Jardim (tel 291 984 937) and Moinho Rent-a-Car (tel 291 982 780).

A more common way of travelling between the islands is by ferry, operated by Porto Santo Line (tel 291 210 300; www.portosantoline.pt), which sails once a day from Funchal, usually at 8am, and back around 7pm (there are two departures a day on Fridays and Sundays in August and on Sunday from mid-July). Return summer fares start at €51.50, with 50 per cent discount for children aged 5–11, and free for under-5s (though they must be issued with a ticket). The crossing takes around 2 hours 15 minutes. Porto Santo Line also operates day cruises, including golfing packages that include transport to the Porto Santo course ($\triangleright$ 37).

ENTRY REQUIREMENTS

As an autonomous region of Portugal, Madeira is part of the EU, so holders of EU passports do not require a visa. Citizens of Australia, Canada, New Zealand and the USA do not require a visa for stays of up to 90 days. Other nationalities should check with their nearest Portuguese embassy. Passengers on flights to and from Portugal need to supply advance passenger information (API)–full name, nationality, date of birth and passport number. This must normally be supplied when booking your trip, online or via your travel agent.
● Visa section, Portuguese Consulate General, 3 Portland Place, London W1; tel: 020 7291 3770

BAGGAGE ALLOWANCES

Budget airlines flying to Madeira (easyJet, Jet2, Air Berlin) have strict weight limits on baggage and may charge a fee for every piece you want to check in. Most airlines allow only one piece of hand luggage on board and this must not exceed certain dimensions. Always check limits before you set off for the airport as charges for excess weight are high.

Getting Around

Madeira is not the most disabled-friendly destination in the world. Extremely steep hills, uneven cobbles, numerous flights of steps and lack of facilities in all but the most expensive hotels make for a difficult experience. However, facilities are improving with the building of new wheelchair-friendly promenades, hotel ramps and low-slung buses (in Funchal), and Madeira's airport has been renovated with disabled passengers firmly in mind. The Golden Residence (www.goldenresidencehotel.com) is the first completely barrier-free hotel on Madeira; more should follow.

MAPS

Free maps of Madeira and Funchal are available from tourist offices and hotel receptions. Recommended maps for those exploring the island by car include those published by the AA (1:50,000). Hikers and drivers should get a copy of the definitive *Madeira Car Tours and Walks* (John and Pat Underwood, Sunflower Books), which contains detailed maps not freely available elsewhere.

BUSES

With no railway on the island, bus is the only way to get around if you don't want the expense and hassle of hiring a car. The service is cheap, easy to use and efficient, and timetables are normally designed to make a day trip from Funchal to anywhere on the island feasible. Five bus companies make sure things keep moving on Madeira. Horários do Funchal (www.horariosdofunchal. pt) operates the capital's fleet of yellow buses; Carros de São Gonçalo (www.horariosdofunchal. pt) serves the island's west and north (Machico, Santana, Camacha); Empresa de Automóveis do Caniço (www.eacl.pt) shuttles between Funchal and Caniço; Rodoeste (www.rodoeste.pt) serves points west (Ribeira Brava, Porto Moniz) and SAM (www.sam.pt) runs services to Machico, the airport and Caniçal.

All buses operating across the island run to or from Funchal and all depart from the bus station at the eastern end of Funchal's Avenida do Mar. Tickets for 'inter-city' services can be bought from kiosks at the station and along Avenida do Mar, or from the driver when you board. The Portuguese word for bus stop is *paragem*, a sign you will see many times as your bus takes the slow route between Funchal and your destination (hardly any buses use the southern motorway).

For Funchal buses, it's best to buy a day pass (€3) from a machine before boarding. Useful routes in Funchal include bus 31 to the Botanical Gardens, bus 6 to the Lido, bus 23 from Livramento (end of the toboggan run) to the city centre, and buses 20 and 21 to Monte; bus numbers for other sights as well as restaurants and some hotels are provided in the practical details following the descriptions of sights and establishments. City buses operate from around 7am to 11pm.

DRIVING

The majority of visitors to Madeira hire a car for the duration of their stay and this is the quickest and most convenient way of seeing the island.

Negotiating Madeira's sometimes almost vertical roads can take some practice, so if you're not a confident driver, or have problems with hill starts or steep drops, save yourself a lot of stress by taking the bus or an organized tour. Car rental rates are cheap, starting at around €100 a week, with local companies tending to be slightly better value than the well-known international names. Drivers should carry their ID, licence and rental documents at all times.

Rules of the road:

● Traffic drives on the right.

● The speed limit is 50kph (30mph) in urban areas, 90kph (55mph) out of town and 120kph (75mph) on the motorway.

● International road signs are used.

● Watch out for Funchal's frequent pedestrian crossings and none-too-bright traffic lights.

TAXIS

Madeira has more taxis than it needs and picking one up at a rank or hailing one in the street is never a problem, even in the remotest of places. All taxis are yellow with a blue stripe, and ageing Mercedes seem to dominate the fleet. There are often flat fees for longer trips, especially to the airport (around €30 from the hotel zone) and these are posted in the vehicle. If you want to hire a taxi for a day or half-day, negotiate with the driver. For journeys around town, the driver will use the meter: the flag fall is between €1.70 and €2, after which the meter adds €0.51 per kilometre. To book a taxi in advance in Funchal, call 291 220 911 or 291 222 000.

CABLE CARS

The *teleféricos* up to Monte and across from Monte to the botanical gardens are a tourist attraction as well as a vital piece of the island's transport infrastructure. There are others at Garajau and Santana. The journey is exhilarating, with some spectacular views along the way. However, this is also a fairly pricey way to travel, with the adult fare for Monte–Funchal, for example, costing €10.

PARKING AND FUEL

● Parking in Funchal is strictly controlled and all parking in the city centre is paid. The handiest car park is the multi-storey near the lower cable car station at the eastern end of Avenida do Mar.

● Across the rest of the island, you'll fine ample and inexpensive car parks and it's usually possible to park on the street for free.

● Petrol stations, found in every coastal town, are a mix of self-service and attendant service. Most hire cars run on lead-free petrol *(gasolina)* from the green pump.

● The petrol station on Funchal's Avenida do Infante is open 24 hours.

TOURS

Group coach tours and guided walks are a convenient and stress-free way of seeing the island. Avoid the east–west full day tour as you'll spend most of the day cooped up on the coach. Instead, choose either an east or west island tour, or specific destinations such as Curral das Freiras or a *levada* walk.

Essential Facts

EMERGENCY NUMBERS

● Fire, police and ambulance
☎ 112

MONEY

Euro notes come in denominations of 5, 10, 20, 50, 100, 200 and 500. Coins come in denominations of 1, 2, 5, 10, 20 and 50 cents, and 1 and 2 euros. Credit and debit cards are widely accepted though not in markets, shops outside Funchal and guesthouses. ATMs have instructions in English. Using a debit card in an ATM generally works out cheaper than changing cash in banks and hotels, but you will be charged a flat fee for each transaction, so making a couple of large withdrawals will be cheaper than many small ones.

5 euros

10 euros

50 euros

100 euros

CUSTOMS ALLOWANCES

● When travelling from an EU country (except Estonia, Latvia, Lithuania, Bulgaria and Romania) there are no limits on the amount of goods you can bring into Portugal providing they are for personal use.
● Duty-free limits for travellers from countries outside the EU are 200 cigarettes or 100 cigarillos or 50 cigars or 250g of tobacco; 1 litre of spirits over 22 per cent or 2 litres of spirits up to 22 per cent; 2 litres of wine; 50g of perfume and 250ml of eau de toilette; gifts to the value of €175.

ELECTRICITY

● Current is 220 volts AC (50 cycles).
● The island uses standard European sockets for plugs with two round pins.
● Hotel kiosks sell adaptors.

EMBASSIES AND CONSULATES

● UK: Rua da Alfândega 10, Room 3C, tel 91 212 860.
● USA: Rua da Alfândega 10, room 2A/B, tel 291 235 636.
● Germany: Largo do Phelps 6, tel 291 220 338.

MAIL

● Post boxes are red and marked Correio.
● A postcard to the UK/Europe requires a €0.68 stamp.

MEDICAL TREATMENT

● Funchal's large hospital (Avenida Luís de Camões, tel 291 705 600) is just north of the hotel zone.
● For information on the EHIC, see page 116.
● When closed, pharmacies *(farmácia)*, indicated by an illuminated green cross, post details of out-of-hours services on the door.

OPENING HOURS

● Most shops are open Mon–Fri 9–7, Sat 9–1; some close for lunch.

● Funchal's main post office (Avenida Zarco 9) is open Mon–Fri 8.30–8, Sat 9–12.30. Other offices keep similar hours but are not open on Saturdays.

● Banking hours are Mon–Fri 8.30–3.

● Museum opening times vary from place to place. Many take a long break in the afternoon and are closed one day in the week.

PUBLIC HOLIDAYS

● 1 Jan, Easter (Good Friday and Easter Monday) in Mar/Apr, 25 Apr, 1 May, 10 Jun, 15 Aug, 5 Oct, 1 Nov, 1 Dec, 8 Dec, 15 Dec.

SENSIBLE PRECAUTIONS

● Crime is low. In fact, Madeira is one of the safest places on the planet.

● Avoid sunstroke on the coast by wearing a hat and drinking plenty of fluids.

● Take warm clothing and food and water if heading into the mountains.

● When walking the *levadas*, take a torch and mobile phone and plan to finish before dark.

SMOKING

● Smoking is banned in all public places.

TELEPHONES

● Mobile coverage on the coast is good, and extensive inland. Mobiles from the EU work normally on Madeira; phones from other parts of the world may not be compatible. Check the costs and coverage with your network provider before arriving in Madeira.

● Phone cards *(cartão de telefone)* for public phones can be bought at cafés, tobacconists and post offices.

TELEPHONE CODES

● To phone Madeira from abroad, use the Portuguese code (00351).

● To phone abroad from Madeira, dial the following code then the subscriber number, omitting the first zero: UK 0044; Ireland 00353; Germany 0049; USA and Canada 001.

MEDIA

● In addition to the Portuguese press, Funchal newsagents stock British, German and other daily newspapers, with editions often appearing in racks on the day of publication. *The Brit* is an excellent English-language newspaper containing features on all kinds of Madeira-related topics. *The Best Guide Madeira*, an annual listings magazine (normally free), comes out in January; it is packed with island info. Almost all hotels have satellite television, with channels such as BBC World, Sky and CNN as standard. For the latest English Premier League game or Champions League match (or rugby, cricket and F1), Funchal has several bars showing major games on big screens.

TIPPING

● Tips in restaurants, cafés, bars and taxis are usually rounded up to the nearest euro or, for good service, add up to 10 per cent.

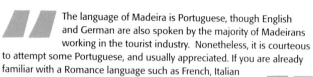

Language

The language of Madeira is Portuguese, though English and German are also spoken by the majority of Madeirans working in the tourist industry. Nonetheless, it is courteous to attempt some Portuguese, and usually appreciated. If you are already familiar with a Romance language such as French, Italian or Spanish, you'll find it fairly easy to understand its written form; understanding its spoken form is a little more difficult.

USEFUL WORDS AND PHRASES

yes/no	*sim/não*
please	*por favor*
thank you	*obrigado* (said by a man), *obrigada* (said by a woman)
hello	*olá*
goodbye	*adeus*
good morning	*bom dia*
good afternoon	*boa tarde*
goodnight	*boa noite*
excuse me	*com licença*
I'm sorry	*desculpe*
how much?	*quanto?*
where	*onde*
big/little	*grande/pequeno*
inexpensive	*barato*
expensive	*caro*
today	*hoje*
tomorrow	*amanhã*
yesterday	*ontem*
open/closed	*aberto/fechado*
men	*homens*
women	*senhoras*
I don't understand	*Não compreendo*
How much is it?	*Quanto custa?*
At what time…?	*A que horas…?*
Please help me	*Ajude-me por favor*
Do you speak English?	*Fala inglês?*
How are you?	*Como está?*
Fine, thank you	*Bem obrigado/a*
My name is…	*Chamo-me…*
I don't speak Portuguese	*Não falo português*

NUMBERS

0	*zero*
1	*um*
2	*dois*
3	*três*
4	*quatro*
5	*cinco*
6	*seis*
7	*sete*
8	*oito*
9	*nove*
10	*dez*
11	*onze*
12	*doze*
13	*treze*
14	*catorze*
15	*quinze*
16	*dezasseis*
17	*dezassete*
18	*dezoito*
19	*dezanove*
50	*vinte*
100	*cem*
500	*quinhentos*

ACCOMMODATION

Does that include breakfast?	*Está incluido o pequeno almoço?*
balcony	*varanda*
air-conditioning	*ar condicionado*
bathroom	*casa de banho*
chambermaid	*camareira*
hot water	*água quente*
key	*chave*
lift	*elevador*
room	*quarto*
room service	*serviço de quarto*
shower	*duche*
telephone	*telefone*
towel	*toalha*

GETTING AROUND

airport	*aeroporto*
boat	*barco*
bus station	*estação de camionetas*
coach	*autocarro*
car	*automóvel*
square	*praça*
street	*rua*
taxi rank	*praça de táxis*
train	*comboio*
station	*estação*

EMERGENCIES

help	*socorro*
stop	*pare*
stop that thief	*apanhe o ladrão*
police	*polícia*
fire	*fogo*
leave me alone	*deixe-me em paz*
I've lost my purse/wallet	*Perdi o meu porta-moedas/a minha carteira*
Could you call a doctor quickly?	*Podia chamar um médico depressa?*
hospital	*hospital*

IN THE RESTAURANT

alcohol	*alcool*
beer	*cerveja*
bill	*conta*
bread	*pão*
café	*café*
coffee	*café*
dinner	*jantar*
lunch	*almoço*
menu	*menú/ ementa*
milk	*leite*
pepper	*pimenta*
salt	*sal*
table	*mesa*
tea	*chá*
waiter	*empregado/ au*

DAYS OF THE WEEK

Sunday	*Domingo*
Monday	*Segunda-feira*
Tuesday	*Terça-feira*
Wednesday	*Quarta-feira*
Thursday	*Quinta-feira*
Friday	*Sexta-feira*
Saturday	*Sábado*

Timeline

COLUMBUS CONNECTION

Essential viewing on Porto Santo is the house in which Christopher Columbus is said to have lived. He arrived in the archipelago in 1478 as a 27-year-old sugar-purchaser and befriended the governor of Porto Santo, Bartolomeu Perestrelo, soon after marrying his daughter, Dona Felipa. Sadly, Dona Felipa died shortly after giving birth, and the child died soon after. In 1480 Columbus returned to Europe and the rest, as they say, is history.

Left to right: statue of Columbus, who once lived on the island; the parish church in Machico, where Europeans first set foot on Madeira; statue of Zarco, who claimed Madeira for Portugal; Fortaleza de São Tiago, Funchal; statue of Teixeira in Machico

20 million BC A volcanic eruption pushes the island above sea level.

AD 77 Madeira is mentioned by Pliny the Elder in his *Naturalis Historia*, in which he dubs the archipelago the 'Purple Isles'.

1351 A Genoese map includes the Isola di Lolegname (Wooded Island) along with Porto Santo and Deserta, the other islands of the archipelago.

1370s English castaway Robert Machin and his wife Anne of Hereford are thought to have landed at Machico.

1418 Blown off course while exploring the coast of Africa, Portuguese navigators João Gonçalves Zarco and Tristão Vaz Teixeira drop anchor near Porto Santo.

1419 Zarco claims Madeira for Portugal.

1420s Zarco and Teixeira become the island's first governors, Zarco in the east, Teixeira in the west.

1452 The island's sub-tropical climate and fertile volcanic soil are found to be ideal for growing sugar cane. Madeira becomes a major exporter of sugar.

1478 Christopher Columbus marries the daughter of the governor of Porto Santo and settles briefly on the island.

1566 French pirates raid Funchal, by then the third largest city in Portugal.

1580 Portugal comes under Spanish rule, drawing Madeira into a war between Spain and England. English ships attack Funchal.

1640 The Portuguese regain independence.

1662 Charles II of England marries Catherine of Braganza, daughter of Portuguese King João IV. Trade between the British Isles and Madeira flourishes; many British merchants set up shop on the island.

1768 Captain Cook calls in at Madeira on his first voyage of discovery.

1851 Madeira's vines are devastated by mildew. The wine industry takes years to recover.

1964 Madeira's airport opens, ending centuries of isolation.

1974 The 'Carnation Revolution' rids Portugal of dictatorship.

1976 Madeira becomes an autonomous region of Portugal.

1997 The southern motorway opens.

2010 In February, Funchal is hit by huge floods. Lives are lost and buildings damaged in the deluge and mudslides.

HERE COME THE BRITS

From Robert Machin, who some claim beat Zarco to being the first person to set foot on Madeira, to the latest easyJet flight to land at the airport, the British have long had a close relationship with the island. The British still dominate the wine trade, Winston Churchill made several visits, and the British launched the island's tourist industry in the 19th century. Many expat Brits call Madeira home and even have their own English Church in Funchal (▷ 43).

MODERNIZING MADEIRA

Madeira's south coast is almost unrecognizable from just two decades ago. EU-funded infrastructure such as flashy new promenades, a new motorway, an expanded airport and Funchal's new cable car system have improved people's lives dramatically.

Index

TWINPACK
Madeira

WRITTEN BY Marc Di Duca
COVER DESIGN Catherine Murray
DESIGN WORK Lesley Mitchell
INDEXER Marie Lorimer
IMAGE RETOUCHING AND REPRO Sarah Montgomery
PROJECT EDITOR Dorothy Stannard
SERIES EDITOR Marie-Claire Jefferies

Colour separation by AA Digital Department
Printed and bound by Leo Paper Products, China

A CIP catalogue record for this book is available from the British Library.

ISBN 978-0-7495-6806-1

We have tried to ensure accuracy in this guide, but things do change, so please
let us know if you have any comments at travelguides@theAA.com.

Published by AA Publishing, a trading name of AA Media Limited, whose
registered office is Fanum House, Basing View, Basingstoke, Hampshire
RG21 4EA. Registered number 06112600.

Front cover image: AA/C Sawyer
Back cover images: (i) AA/J Wyand; (ii) AA/C Sawyer; (iii) AA/J Wyand;
(iv) AA/C Sawyer

A04027
Maps in this title produced from mapping © MAIRDUMONT / Falk Verlag 2011

The Automobile Association would like to thank the following photographers, companies and picture libraries for their assistance in the preparation of this book.

Abbreviations for the pictures credits are as follows – (t) top; (b) bottom; (c) centre; (l) left; (r) right; (AA) AA World Travel Library.

1 AA/C Sawyer; 2t–18t AA/C Sawyer; 4b AA/C Sawyer; 5b AA/C Sawyer; 6cl AA/C Sawyer; 6c Madeira Story Centre; 6cr AA/C Sawyer; 6bl AA/C Sawyer; 6bcl AA/C Sawyer; 6bcr AA/J Wyand; 6br AA/C Sawyer; 7cl AA/C Sawyer; 7c AA/J Wyand; 7cr AA/J Wyand; 7bl AA/C Sawyer; 7bc AA/C Sawyer; 7br AA/C Sawyer; 10ct AA/C Sawyer; 10c AA/C Sawyer; 10/11 AA/C Sawyer; 11ct AA/J Wyand; 11c AA/C Sawyer; 12i AA/J Wyand; 12ii AA/C Sawyer; 12iii AA/M Wells; 12iv AA/J Wyand; 13i AA/M Bonnet; 13ii Brand X Pics; 13iii AA/C Sawyer; 13iv AA/C Sawyer; 13v AA/M Wells; 14i AA/C Sawyer; 14ii AA/J Wyand; 14iii AA/M Wells; 14iv AA/C Sawyer; 15b AA/C Sawyer; 16i AA/J Wyand; 16ii allOver photography/Alamy; 16iii Courtesy of Choupana Hills Resort & Spa; 16iv AA/C Sawyer; 17i AA/A Belcher; 17ii Courtesy of The Reid's Palace Hotel; 17iii AA/C Sawyer; 17iv AA/J Wyand; 18i AA/C Sawyer; 18ii Courtesy of the Madeira Theme Park; 18iii AA/C Sawyer; 18iv AA/C Sawyer; 19i AA/C Sawyer; 19ii AA/P Baker; 19iii AA/C Sawyer; 19iv AA/C Sawyer; 19v AA/P Baker; 20/21 AA/J Wyand; 24/25 Hackenberg-Photo-Cologne/Alamy; 25t Hackenberg-Photo-Cologne/Alamy; 25b Hackenberg-Photo-Cologne/Alamy; 26l AA/P Baker; 26r AA/P Baker; 27l imagebroker/Alamy; 27r AA/J Wyand; 28/29 Courtesy of the Museu de Arte Sacra, Funchal; 29 AA/J Wyand; 30l AA/C Sawyer; 30r AA/C Sawyer; 30/31 AA/C Sawyer; 31t AA/C Sawyer; 31b AA/C Sawyer; 32l AA/C Sawyer; 32r AA/C Sawyer; 33-37t AA/C Sawyer; 33bl AA/C Sawyer; 33br AA/C Sawyer; 34b Courtesy of the Madeira Story Centre; 35bl AA/J Wyand; 35br AA/J Wyand; 36b AA/C Sawyer; 37b AA/J Wyand; 38 AA/C Sawyer; 39 AA/C Sawyer; 40-42, 105t AA/C Sawyer; 43-44, 91, 105b Porto Santo Diving Centre; 45-48, 62, 78, 92, 106 AA/C Sawyer; 49 AA/J Wyand; 52l AA/J Wyand; 52c AA/J Wyand; 52r AA/C Sawyer; 53l AA/C Sawyer; 53r AA/C Sawyer; 54 AA/C Sawyer; 55 Pepbaix/Alamy; 56 WoodyStock/Alamy; 57tl AA/J Wyand; 57tr AA/J Wyand; 57b AA/J Wyand; 58l AA/J Wyand; 58r AA/C Sawyer; 59l AA/C Sawyer; 59r AA/C Sawyer; 60l AA/C Sawyer; 60c AA/C Sawyer; 60r AA/C Sawyer; 61l John Keates/Alamy; 61r AA/C Sawyer; 63 AA/C Sawyer; 66 AA/C Sawyer; 66/67 ©mauritius images GmbH/Alamy 68l AA/C Sawyer; 68c AA/J Wyand; 68r AA/C Sawyer; 69l AA/C Sawyer; 69r AA/C Sawyer; 70/71 Paul Maguire/Alamy; 71 Paul Maguire/Alamy; 72l AA/C Sawyer; 72r AA/C Sawyer; 73t-75t AA/C Sawyer; 73b AA/C Sawyer; 74bl Courtesy of The Madeira Theme Park; 74br AA/J Wyand; 75b AA/C Sawyer; 76 AA/C Sawyer; 77 AA/P Baker; 79 AA/C Sawyer; 82l AA/C Sawyer; 82r AA/C Sawyer; 83l AA/J Wyand; 83r Pepbaix/Alamy; 84l AA/J Wyand; 84/85t AA/C Sawyer; 84/85b AA/C Sawyer; 85t AA/P Baker; 85b AA/C Sawyer; 86-87t AA/J Wyand; 86b AA/J Wyand; 87l AA/C Sawyer; 87r AA/J Wyand; 88 AA/C Sawyer; 89 AA/C Sawyer; 90 AA/C Sawyer; 93 AA/C Sawyer; 96/97 blickwinkel/Alamy; 97 AA/J Wyand; 98/99 Werner Otto/Alamy; 99t AA/C Sawyer; 99b AA/P Baker; 100/101 AA/C Sawyer; 101t AA/C Sawyer; 101b AA/C Sawyer; 102 AA/C Sawyer; 103t AA/C Sawyer; 103bl AA/P Baker; 103br AA/J Wyand; 104 AA/J Wyand; 105t AA/J Wyand;107 AA/C Sawyer; 108-112t AA/C Sawyer; 108i Courtesy of The Vine Hotel; 108ii Courtesy of Hotel Windsor; 108iii Courtesy of Porto Bay Hotel, Porto Santa Maria; 108iv Courtesy of Quinta do Serrado; 108v Courtesy of Quinta Splendida; 113 AA/C Sawyer; 114-123t AA/P Baker; 120 European Central Bank; 124l AA/C Sawyer; 124r AA/C Sawyer; 125l AA/J Wyand; 125c AA/C Sawyer; 125r AA/C Sawyer

Every effort has been made to trace the copyright holders, and we apologise in advance for any accidental errors. We would be happy to apply any corrections in the following edition of this publication.

SAM #81 CURRAL das FREIRAS
11 AM — JOURNEY = 1 hrs TICKET
ON BUS PP each WAY +- €2.75
TERMINUS NEXT TO CABLECAR